For Erika, life has been a journey – a time of dazzling achievements and heartbreaking situations. She is a dreamer, working hard to pursue her dream of exploring the world, as for her: "Our thoughts are powerful and we are bigger than our dreams as it must always exceed our capacity to achieve them." She has faced struggles mainly by herself, all the while on a search for self-discovery and happiness.

She has turned the lessons she learned on her journey into *Be Inspired,* an overpowering 365-day collection of her most honest, brave, and hopeful insights. These are her own words, along with quotes that inspire her as personal reflection and goals for life.

This is a book for everyone, everywhere, on their own journey who needs comfort, motivation, and a reason to be inspired every day.

I dedicate this book to my soulmate and love of my life, my husband Marwan and our son Mansoor. You both mean everything to me. I feel so blessed to have you in my life.

Erika Cristina

BE INSPIRED

365 Daily's Motivational for The Year

Cintia,
Much Love ♡
Big hug,
Erika ☺
NOV/DUBAI

AUSTIN MACAULEY PUBLISHERS™
LONDON * CAMBRIDGE * NEW YORK * SHARJAH

Copyright © Erika Cristina (2021)

The right of Erika Cristina to be identified as author of this work has been asserted by the author in accordance with Federal Law No. (7) of UAE, Year 2002, Concerning Copyrights and Neighboring Rights.

All rights reserved. No part of this publication may be reproduced, stored in a retrieval system, or transmitted in any form or by any means, electronic, mechanical, photocopying, recording, or otherwise, without the prior permission of the publishers.

Any person who commits any unauthorized act in relation to this publication may be liable to legal prosecution and civil claims for damages.

The age group that matches the content of the books has been classified according to the age classification system issued by the National Media Council.

ISBN – 9789948834069 – (Paperback)
ISBN – 9789948834052 – (E-Book)

Application Number: MC-10-01-5813291
Age Classification: E

Printer Name: Al Nisr Publishing LLC
Printer Address: Dubai, United Arab Emirates

First Published (2021)
AUSTIN MACAULEY PUBLISHERS FZE
Sharjah Publishing City
P.O Box [519201]
Sharjah, UAE
www.austinmacauley.ae
+971 655 95 202

A special thanks to my best friend Cristine. Your support and friendship are so precious to me. Somehow you stay with me no matter what, and that makes me feel so happy and special. Thank you for being the best friend in the world.

Table of Contents

Introduction	23
January	25
Day One: January 1	27
Day Two: January 2	28
Day Three: January 3	29
Day Four: January 4	30
Day Five: January 5	31
Day Six: January 6	32
Day Seven: January 7	33
Day Eight: January 8	34
Day Nine: January 9	35
Day Ten: January 10	36
Day Eleven: January 11	37
Day Twelve: January 12	38
Day Thirteen: January 13	39
Day Fourteen: January 14	40
Day Fifteen: January 15	41
Day Sixteen: January 16	42
Day Seventeen: January 17	43
Day Eighteen: January 18	44
Day Nineteen: January 19	45
Day Twenty: January 20	46
Day Twenty-One: January 21	47
Day Twenty-Two: January 22	48
Day Twenty-Three: January 23	49

Day Twenty-Four: January 24	*50*
Day Twenty-Five: January 25	*51*
Day Twenty-Six: January 26	*52*
Day Twenty-Seven: January 27	*53*
Day Twenty-Eight: January 28	*54*
Day Twenty-Nine: January 29	*55*
Day Thirty: January 30	*56*
Day Thirty-One: January 31	*57*
February	**59**
Day Thirty-Two: February 1	*61*
Day Thirty-Three: February 2	*62*
Day Thirty-Four: February 3	*63*
Day Thirty-Five: February 4	*64*
Day Thirty-Six: February 5	*65*
Day Thirty-Seven: February 6	*66*
Day Thirty-Eight: February 7	*67*
Day Thirty-Nine: February 8	*68*
Day Forty: February 9	*69*
Day Forty-One: February 10	*70*
Day Forty-Two: February 11	*71*
Day Forty-Three: February 12	*72*
Day Forty-Four: February 13	*73*
Day Forty-Five: February 14	*74*
Day Forty-Six: February 15	*75*
Day Forty-Seven: February 16	*76*
Day Forty-Eight: February 17	*77*
Day Forty-Nine: February 18	*78*
Day Fifty: February 19	*79*
Day Fifty-One: February 20	*80*
Day Fifty-Two: February 21	*81*
Day Fifty-Three: February 22	*82*

Day Fifty-Four: February 23	83
Day Fifty-Five: February 24	84
Day Fifty-Six: February 25	85
Day Fifty-Seven: February 26	86
Day Fifty-Eight: February 27	87
Day Fifty-Nine: February 28	88
March	**89**
Day Sixty: March 1	91
Day Sixty-One: March 2	92
Day Sixty-Two: March 3	93
Day Sixty-Three: March 4	94
Day Sixty-Four: March 5	95
Day Sixty-Five: March 6	96
Day Sixty-Six: March 7	97
Day Sixty-Seven: March 8	98
Day Sixty-Eight: March 9	99
Day Sixty-Nine: March 10	100
Day Seventy: March 11	101
Day Seventy-One: March 12	102
Day Seventy-Two: March 13	103
Day Seventy-Three: March 14	104
Day Seventy-Four: March 15	105
Day Seventy-Five: March 16	106
Day Seventy-Six: March 17	107
Day Seventy-Seven: March 18	108
Day Seventy-Eight: March 19	109
Day Seventy-Nine: March 20	110
Day Eighty: March 21	111
Day Eighty-One: March 22	112
Day Eighty-Two: March 23	113
Day Eighty-Three: March 24	114

Day Eighty-Four: March 25   *115*

Day Eighty-Five: March 26   *116*

Day Eighty-Six: March 27   *117*

Day Eighty-Seven: March 28   *118*

Day Eighty-Eight: March 29   *119*

Day Eighty-Nine: March 30   *120*

Day Ninety: March 31   *121*

April   **123**

Day Ninety-One: April 1   *125*

Day Ninety-Two: April 2   *126*

Day Ninety-Three: April 3   *127*

Day Ninety-Four: April 4   *128*

Day Ninety-Five: April 5   *129*

Day Ninety-Six: April 6   *130*

Day Ninety-Seven: April 7   *131*

Day Ninety-Eight: April 8   *132*

Day Ninety-Nine: April 9   *133*

Day One-Hundred: April 10   *134*

Day One-Hundred-and-One: April 11   *135*

Day One-Hundred-and-Two: April 12   *136*

Day One-Hundred-and-Three: April 13   *137*

Day One-Hundred-and-Four: April 14   *138*

Day One-Hundred-and-Five: April 15   *139*

Day One-Hundred-and-Six: April 16   *140*

Day One-Hundred-and-Seven: April 17   *141*

Day One-Hundred-and-Eight: April 18   *142*

Day One-Hundred-and-Nine: April 19   *143*

Day One-Hundred-and-Ten: April 20   *144*

Day One-Hundred-and-Eleven: April 21   *145*

Day One-Hundred-and-Twelve: April 22   *146*

Day One-Hundred-and-Thirteen: April 23   *147*

Day One-Hundred-and-Fourteen: April 24   *148*

Day One-Hundred-and-Fifteen: April 25   *149*

Day One-Hundred-and-Sixteen: April 26   *150*

Day One-Hundred-and-Seventeen: April 27   *151*

Day One-Hundred-and-Eighteen: April 28   *152*

Day One-Hundred-and-Nineteen: April 29   *153*

Day One-Hundred-and-Twenty: April 30   *154*

May   **155**

Day One-Hundred-and-Twenty-One: May 1   *157*

Day One-Hundred-and-Twenty-Two: May 2   *158*

Day One-Hundred-and-Twenty-Three: May 3   *159*

Day One-Hundred-and-Twenty-Four: May 4   *160*

Day One-Hundred-and-Twenty-Five: May 5   *161*

Day One-Hundred-and-Twenty-Six: May 6   *162*

Day One-Hundred-and-Twenty-Seven: May 7   *163*

Day One-Hundred-and-Twenty-Eight: May 8   *164*

Day One-Hundred-and-Twenty-Nine: May 9   *165*

Day One-Hundred-and-Thirty: May 10   *166*

Day One-Hundred-and-Thirty-One: May 11   *167*

Day One-Hundred-and-Thirty-Two: May 12   *168*

Day One-Hundred-and-Thirty-Three: May 13   *169*

Day One-Hundred-and-Thirty-Four: May 14   *170*

Day One-Hundred-and-Thirty-Five: May 15   *171*

Day One-Hundred-and-Thirty-Six: May 16   *172*

Day One-Hundred-and-Thirty-Seven: May 17   *173*

Day One-Hundred-and-Thirty-Eight: May 18   *174*

Day One-Hundred-and-Thirty-Nine: May 19   *175*

Day One-Hundred-and-Forty: May 20   *176*

Day One-Hundred-and-Forty-One: May 21   *177*

Day One-Hundred-and-Forty-Two: May 22   *178*

Day One-Hundred-and-Forty-Three: May 23   *179*

Day One-Hundred-and-Forty-Four: May 24   *180*

Day One-Hundred-and-Forty-Five: May 25   *181*

Day One-Hundred-and-Forty-Six: May 26   *182*

Day One-Hundred-and-Forty-Seven: May 27   *183*

Day One-Hundred-and-Forty-Eight: May 28   *184*

Day One-Hundred-and-Forty-Nine: May 29   *185*

Day One-Hundred-and-Fifty: May 30   *186*

Day One-Hundred-and-Fifty-One: May 31   *187*

June   **189**

Day One-Hundred-and-Fifty-Two: June 1   *191*

Day One-Hundred-and-Fifty-Three: June 2   *192*

Day One-Hundred-and-Fifty-Four: June 3   *193*

Day One-Hundred-and-Fifty-Five: June 4   *194*

Day One-Hundred-and-Fifty-Six: June 5   *195*

Day One-Hundred-and-Fifty-Seven: June 6   *196*

Day One-Hundred-And-Fifty-Eight: June 7   *197*

Day One-Hundred-and-Fifty-Nine: June 8   *198*

Day One-Hundred-and-Sixty: June 9   *199*

Day One-Hundred-and-Sixty-One: June 10   *200*

Day One-Hundred-and-Sixty-Two: June 11   *201*

Day One-Hundred-and-Sixty-Three: June 12   *202*

Day One-Hundred-and-Sixty-Four: June 13   *203*

Day One-Hundred-and-Sixty-Five: June 14   *204*

Day One-Hundred-and-Sixty-Six: June 15   *205*

Day One-Hundred-and-Sixty-Seven: June 16   *206*

Day One-Hundred-and-Sixty-Eight: June 17   *207*

Day One-Hundred-and-Sixty-Nine: June 18   *208*

Day One-Hundred-and-Seventy: June 19   *209*

Day One-Hundred-and-Seventy-One: June 20   *210*

Day One-Hundred-And-Seventy-Two: June 21   *211*

Day One-Hundred-And-Seventy-Three: June 22   *212*

Day One-Hundred-and-Seventy-Four: June 23	*213*
Day One-Hundred-and-Seventy-Five: June 24	*214*
Day One-Hundred-and-Seventy-Six: June 25	*215*
Day One-Hundred-and-Seventy-Seven: June 26	*216*
Day One-Hundred-and-Seventy-Eight: June 27	*217*
Day One-Hundred-and-Seventy-Nine: June 28	*218*
Day One-Hundred-and-Eighty: June 29	*219*
Day One-Hundred-and-Eighty-One: June 30	*220*
July	**221**
Day One-Hundred-And-Eighty-Two: July 1	*223*
Day One-Hundred-and-Eighty-Three: July 2	*224*
Day One-Hundred-and-Eighty-Four: July 3	*225*
Day One-Hundred-and-Eighty-Five: July 4	*226*
Day One-Hundred-and-Eighty-Six: July 5	*227*
Day One-Hundred-and-Eighty-Seven: July 6	*228*
Day One-Hundred-and-Eighty-Eight: July 7	*229*
Day One-Hundred-and-Eighty-Nine: July 8	*230*
Day One-Hundred-and-Ninety: July 9	*231*
Day One-Hundred-and-Ninety-One: July 10	*232*
Day One-Hundred-and-Ninety-Two: July 11	*233*
Day One-Hundred-and-Ninety-Three: July 12	*234*
Day One-Hundred-and-Ninety-Four: July 13	*235*
Day One-Hundred-and-Ninety-Five: July 14	*236*
Day One-Hundred-and-Ninety-Six: July 15	*237*
Day One-Hundred-and-Ninety-Seven: July 16	*238*
Day One-Hundred-and-Ninety-Eight: July 17	*239*
Day One-Hundred-and-Ninety-Nine: July 18	*240*
Day Two-Hundred: July 19	*241*
Day Two-Hundred-and-One: July 20	*242*
Day Two-Hundred-and-Two: July 21	*243*
Day Two-Hundred-and-Three: July 22	*244*

Day Two-Hundred-and-Four: July 23   *245*

Day Two-Hundred-and-Five: July 24   *246*

Day Two-Hundred-and-Six: July 25   *247*

Day Two-Hundred-and-Seven: July 26   *248*

Day Two-Hundred-and-Eight: July 27   *249*

Day Two-Hundred-and-Nine: July 28   *250*

Day Two-Hundred-and-Ten: July 29   *251*

Day Two-Hundred-and-Eleven: July 30   *252*

Day One-Hundred-and-Twelve: July 31   *253*

August   **255**

Day Two-Hundred-and-Thirteen: August 1   *257*

Day Two-Hundred-and-Fourteen: August 2   *258*

Day Two-Hundred-and-Fifteen: August 3   *259*

Day Two-Hundred-and-Sixteen: August 4   *260*

Day Two-Hundred-and-Seventeen: August 5   *261*

Day Two-Hundred-and-Eighteen: August 6   *262*

Day Two-Hundred-and-Nineteen: August 7   *263*

Day Two-Hundred-and-Twenty: August 8   *264*

Day Two-Hundred-and-Twenty-One: August 9   *265*

Day Two-Hundred-and-Twenty-Two: August 10   *266*

Day Two-Hundred-and-Twenty-Three: August 11   *267*

Day Two-Hundred-and-Twenty-Four: August 12   *268*

Day Two-Hundred-and-Twenty-Five: August 13   *269*

Day Two-Hundred-and-Twenty-Six: August 14   *270*

Day Two-Hundred-and-Twenty-Seven: August 15   *271*

Day Two-Hundred-and-Twenty-Eight: August 16   *272*

Day Two-Hundred-and-Twenty-Nine: August 17   *273*

Day Two-Hundred-and-Thirty: August 18   *274*

Day Two-Hundred-and-Thirty-One: August 19   *275*

Day Two-Hundred-and-Thirty-Two: August 20   *276*

Day Two-Hundred-and-Thirty-Three: August 21   *277*

Day Two-Hundred-and-Thirty-Four: August 22	*278*
Day Two-Hundred-and-Thirty-Five: August 23	*279*
Day Two-Hundred-and-Thirty-Six: August 24	*280*
Day Two-Hundred-and-Thirty-Seven: August 25	*281*
Day Two-Hundred-and-Thirty-Eight: August 26	*282*
Day Two-Hundred-and-Thirty-Nine: August 27	*283*
Day Two-Hundred-and-Forty: August 28	*284*
Day Two-Hundred-and-Forty-One: August 29	*285*
Day Two-Hundred-And-Forty-Two: August 30	*286*
Day Two-Hundred-and-Forty-Three: August 31	*287*
September	**289**
Day Two-Hundred-and-Forty-Four: September 1	*291*
Day Two-Hundred-and-Forty-Five: September 2	*292*
Day Two-Hundred-and-Forty-Six: September 3	*293*
Day Two-Hundred-and-Forty-Seven: September 4	*294*
Day Two-Hundred-and-Forty-Eight: September 5	*295*
Day Two-Hundred-and-Forty-Nine: September 6	*296*
Day Two-Hundred-and-Fifty: September 7	*297*
Day Two-Hundred-and-Fifty-One: September 8	*298*
Day Two-Hundred-and-Fifty-Two: September 9	*299*
Day Two-Hundred-and-Fifty-Three: September 10	*300*
Day Two-Hundred-and-Fifty-Four: September 11	*301*
Day Two-Hundred-and-Fifty-Five: September 12	*302*
Day Two-Hundred-and-Fifty-Six: September 13	*303*
Day Two-Hundred-and-Fifty-Seven: September 14	*304*
Day Two-Hundred-and-Fifty-Eight: September 15	*305*
Day Two-Hundred-and-Fifty-Nine: September 16	*306*
Day Two-Hundred-and-Sixty: September 17	*307*
Day Two-Hundred-and-Sixty-One: September 18	*308*
Day Two-Hundred-and-Sixty-Two: September 19	*309*
Day Two-Hundred-and-Sixty-Three: September 20	*310*

Day Two-Hundred-and-Sixty-Four: September 21   *311*

Day Two-Hundred-and-Sixty-Five: September 22   *312*

Day Two-Hundred-and-Sixty-Six: September 23   *313*

Day Two-Hundred-and-Sixty-Seven: September 24   *314*

Day Two-Hundred-and-Sixty-Eight: September 25   *315*

Day Two-Hundred-and-Sixty-Nine: September 26   *316*

Day Two-Hundred-and-Seventy: September 27   *317*

Day Two-Hundred-and-Seventy-One: September 28   *318*

Day Two-Hundred-and-Seventy-Two: September 29   *319*

Day Two-Hundred-and-Seventy-Three: September 30   *320*

October   **321**

Day Two-Hundred-and-Seventy-Four: October 1   *323*

Day Two-Hundred-and-Seventy-Five: October 2   *324*

Day Two-Hundred-and-Seventy-Six: October 3   *325*

Day Two-Hundred-and-Seventy-Seven: October 4   *326*

Day Two-Hundred-and-Seventy-Eight: October 5   *327*

Day Two-Hundred-and-Seventy-Nine: October 6   *328*

Day Two-Hundred-and-Eighty: October 7   *329*

Day Two-Hundred-and-Eighty-One: October 8   *330*

Day Two-Hundred-and-Eighty-Two: October 9   *331*

Day Two-Hundred-and-Eighty-Three: October 10   *332*

Day Two-Hundred-and-Eighty-Four: October 11   *333*

Day Two-Hundred-and-Eighty-Five: October 12   *334*

Day Two-Hundred-and-Eighty-Six: October 13   *335*

Day Two-Hundred-and-Eighty-Seven: October 14   *336*

Day Two-Hundred-and-Eighty-Eight: October 15   *337*

Day Two-Hundred-and-Eighty-Nine: October 16   *338*

Day Two-Hundred-and-Ninety: October 17   *339*

Day Two-Hundred-and-Ninety-One: October 18   *340*

Day Two-Hundred-and-Ninety-Two: October 19   *341*

Day Two-Hundred-and-Ninety-Three: October 20   *342*

Day Two-Hundred-and-Ninety-Four: October 21 ... *343*
Day Two-Hundred-and-Ninety-Five: October 22 ... *344*
Day Two-Hundred-and-Ninety-Six: October 23 ... *345*
Day Two-Hundred-and-Ninety-Seven: October 24 ... *346*
Day Two-Hundred-and-Ninety-Eight: October 25 ... *347*
Day Two-Hundred-and-Ninety-Nine: October 26 ... *348*
Day Three-Hundred: October 27 ... *349*
Day Three-Hundred-and-One: October 28 ... *350*
Day Three-Hundred-and-Two: October 29 ... *351*
Day Three-Hundred-and-Three: October 30 ... *352*
Day Three-Hundred-and-Four: October 31 ... *353*

November ... **355**

Day Three-Hundred-and-Five: November 1 ... *357*
Day Three-Hundred-and-Six: November 2 ... *358*
Day Three-Hundred-and-Seven: November 3 ... *359*
Day Three-Hundred-and-Eight: November 4 ... *360*
Day Three-Hundred-and-Nine: November 5 ... *361*
Day Three-Hundred-and-Ten: November 6 ... *362*
Day Three-Hundred-and-Eleven: November 7 ... *363*
Day Three-Hundred-and-Twelve: November 8 ... *364*
Day Three-Hundred-and-Thirteen: November 9 ... *365*
Day Three-Hundred-and-Fourteen: November 10 ... *366*
Day Three-Hundred-and-Fifteen: November 11 ... *367*
Day Three-Hundred-and-Sixteen: November 12 ... *368*
Day Three-Hundred-and-Seventeen: November 13 ... *369*
Day Three-Hundred-and-Eighteen: November 14 ... *370*
Day Three-Hundred-and-Nineteen: November 15 ... *371*
Day Three-Hundred-and-Twenty: November 16 ... *372*
Day Three-Hundred-and-Twenty-One: November 17 ... *373*
Day Three-Hundred-and-Twenty-Two: November 18 ... *374*
Day Three-Hundred-and-Twenty-Three: November 19 ... *375*

Day Three-Hundred-and-Twenty-Four: November 20	*376*
Day Three-Hundred-and-Twenty-Five: November 21	*377*
Day Three-Hundred-and-Twenty-Six: November 22	*378*
Day Three-Hundred-and-Twenty-Seven: November 23	*379*
Day Three-Hundred-and-Twenty-Eight: November 24	*380*
Day Three-Hundred-and-Twenty-Nine: November 25	*381*
Day Three-Hundred-and-Thirty: November 26	*382*
Day Three-Hundred-and-Thirty-One: November 27	*383*
Day Three-Hundred-and-Thirty-Two: November 28	*384*
Day Three-Hundred-and-Thirty-Three: November 29	*385*
Day Three-Hundred-and-Thirty-Four: November 30	*386*
December	**387**
Day Three-Hundred-and-Thirty-Five: December 1	*389*
Day Three-Hundred-and-Thirty-Six: December 2	*390*
Day Three-Hundred-and-Thirty-Seven: December 3	*391*
Day Three-Hundred-and-Thirty-Eight: December 4	*392*
Day Three-Hundred-and-Thirty-Nine: December 5	*393*
Day Three-Hundred-and-Forty: December 6	*394*
Day Three-Hundred-and-Forty-One: December 7	*395*
Day Three-Hundred-and-Forty-Two: December 8	*396*
Day Three-Hundred-and-Forty-Three: December 9	*397*
Day Three-Hundred-and-Forty-Four: December 10	*398*
Day Three-Hundred-and-Forty-Five: December 11	*399*
Day Three-Hundred-and-Forty-Six: December 12	*400*
Day Three-Hundred-and-Forty-Seven: December 13	*401*
Day Three-Hundred-and-Forty-Eight: December 14	*402*
Day Three-Hundred-and-Forty-Nine: December 15	*403*
Day Three-Hundred-and-Fifty: December 16	*404*
Day Three-Hundred-and-Fifty-One: December 17	*405*
Day Three-Hundred-and-Fifty-Two: December 18	*406*
Day Three-Hundred-and-Fifty-Three: December 19	*407*

Day Three-Hundred-and-Fifty-Four: December 20	*408*
Day Three-Hundred-and-Fifty-Five: December 21	*409*
Day Three-Hundred-and-Fifty-Six: December 22	*410*
Day Three-Hundred-and-Fifty-Seven: December 23	*411*
Day Three-Hundred-and-Fifty-Eight: December 24	*412*
Day Three-Hundred-and-Fifty-Nine: December 25	*413*
Day Three-Hundred-and-Sixty: December 26	*414*
Day Three-Hundred-and-Sixty-One: December 27	*415*
Day Three-Hundred-and-Sixty-Two: December 28	*416*
Day Three-Hundred-and-Sixty-Three: December 29	*417*
Day Three-Hundred-and-Sixty-Four: December 30	*418*
Day Three-Hundred-and-Sixty-Five: December 31	*419*

Introduction

Dear reader,

I would love to inspire you with some kind-hearted words and a page per day bringing you happiness, strength, and peace. I have been through so many kinds of experiences in life, and the most struggling one was to save my baby's life and mine after I found out about a malignant tumor during my pregnancy just three days after my friend Tatiana got the same diagnosis; our life has changed completely and we are stronger than ever before. There are always going to be highs and lows, heartbreaks and victories, and everything in-between. So sometimes the smallest words can make all the difference, they can sympathize and inspire.

Each day I wake up grateful and remember to count all my blessings, starting from being alive and healthy. Though some days it can be a struggle, it's important to have something that will motivate us, help us to stay positive, and inspire us to keep moving forward.

This book is a collection of my own words, quotes that inspired me, reflections, lessons, experiences, and a full year of amazing goals. As they have and continue to help me tremendously, so would I love to share this special gift from my heart to you. Wherever you are in life, stay strong, be kind, compassionate, brave, love hard and deeply, forgive, and keep smiling from your soul. Remember that you are beautiful!

– ***With love, Erika***

JANUARY

Day One: January 1

When life hands you lemons, make lemonade.

Going through life can have so many bitter experiences attached. An unpleasant day, a bad deal, or even almost going bankrupt. But there is nothing that can't be turned into a positive experience. As the saying goes, when life hands you lemons you make lemonades out of it. This is very true, and you might want to start holding on to the saying more. It has given me the strength to move ahead even while I was going through tight situations, and it taught me more about being positive that any other thing.

GOAL: Be positive about everything around you, no matter how bad they seem. Deliberately stand in front of the mirror for some minutes and repeat the words 'I can do it!' everything is going to be okay soon.

Day Two: January 2

It's not whether you get knocked down, it's whether you get up.

– Henry Miller

I have had to deal with several situations every day, and not everything is a success. However, I have learned that there is no such thing as failure. Instead, I have just discovered one way not to go about solving a problem. Life can be exactly like that, so don't let one failure spoil your chances of many successes. When you fall, get back on, take life by the reins, and ride it like you never fell.

GOAL: Look back at every time you have failed and try to see what went wrong. Then go back, correct it, and be prepared to win.

Day Three: January 3

Dreaming big is not enough, get out and make something happen.

I have had those beautiful daydreams too, those that are filled with swiveling chairs at the pent office with a magnificent view of the city. But I know it's never going to happen if I dream it all day. So I get up and work toward it. One step in the right direction every day will lead you closer and closer to your dream. So don't just sit there and dream, make something happen.

GOAL: Decide to take a step today in the right direction. It could be that proposal you have been putting off, and it could be taking on that task you have been scared of doing.

Day Four: January 4

Whether you think you can or you think you can't, you are right.

– Henry Ford

Attitudes really matter, I learned this long ago. I have been through a lot, and most of the mindset I had didn't do much to lift the bad clouds. But with the right attitude, you can get through a bad day with excellent outcomes. No matter what is going on, don't exude negative attitude, always be positive with a 'can-do' attitude. Remember, you are what you make of yourself.

GOAL: Next time you face a difficult problem, look at it and assure yourself you can do it no matter what.

Day Five: January 5

We may encounter many defeats, but we may not be defeated.

– Maya Angelou

I remember trying so hard to get back up, but the more I tried, the harder I fell. Then I saw this quote, and it strengthened my resolve never to give up. The quote is an eye-opener. Let your resolve never to give up become stronger, and nothing would be able to stop you from becoming what you want.

GOAL: The most certain way to succeed is always to try just one more time. Keep going.

Day Six: January 6

Love yourself more than anyone can love you.

Self-love can never be overrated; you have to love yourself first before anyone can love you. Love your shape, love the way you look, and appreciate everything you are. In fact, this is the key to becoming someone everyone sees, loves, and respects. Not loving yourself enough can cause others to walk all over you, but if you love yourself so much, no relationships, person, or entity would be able to cause you to be sad.

GOAL: Stand in front of the mirror and tell yourself how much you love 'you' for the person you are.

Day Seven: January 7

Yesterday is history, tomorrow is a mystery, and today is a gift…that is why they call it present.

– Master Oogway

Here is one of the best quote from the *Kung Fu Panda* series by DreamWorks animation. We don't have to let what happened yesterday ruin our today; today is a gift we have been given, and we can do whatever we want with it. That is why it is a present. Go after every goal you have for the day and make sure every second counts.

GOAL: Go into the day with a fresh, positive perspective to your outlook on life.

Day Eight: January 8

Trust your heart and follow your instincts.

Your true inner voice is one of the best guides you have. It helped me through many days, and it can help you too. Try to shut out the worries, the debt, or the bills, and let it speak. Its soothing voice can be the key to your happiness. Don't let your fear get the best of you. Get back in touch with the best part of yourself – your inner voice.

    GOAL: Meditate at least 15 minutes today and listen to what your heart tells you.

Day Nine: January 9

Only those who risk going too far can find out how far one can go.

– T.S. Eliot

Holding back can stop you from experiencing all the amazing things that life has to offer. Push boundaries, break through walls, and literally conquer your fear one by one till there is none left.

GOAL: Create a list of the things you are scared of doing, then make sure that you start from your least fears and start working on them one after the other till the list is all done.

Day Ten: January 10

The easiest option is mostly not always the right one.

There will certainly be a lot of times where taking the easy way out would seem like the best option. So you could tell a simple lie, take a little extra paper or add some extra digits to the normal charge, but these things would definitely catch up with you. When it seems like being dishonest is part of the option, think of the long term effect and check yourself. Don't be part of the crowd and do wrong; do what's right even if you would stand alone.

GOAL: No matter how many people around you have a habit of doing the wrong thing, consciously decide not to join them but be an example to them.

Day Eleven: January 11

Reading is to the mind as exercise is to the body.

– Brian Tracy

If you want to keep having fresh ideas and better ways to handle things, then make reading a habit. Just the way exercise makes your body strong and alert, books also help you sharpen your mind. Anyone who reads would certainly be more intelligent, and I'm sure of this because it is something that has helped me through the years. It's important also to read the right set of books, especially ones that have to do with what you want to become.

GOAL: Develop a habit of reading, so check online and look up books that have to do with the business you are going into, your career, or your academics. Buy these books or check them out at the local library if you can't afford them and make sure you read them.

Day Twelve: January 12

The way to get started is to quit talking and begin doing.

– Walt Disney

We have to start somewhere before arriving at the destination we desire. Always remember, your plan and talks won't make things happen, you have to start doing something about them. Through challenges and seemingly difficult situations, I have learned to execute the plans I make rather than just keeping them in a note somewhere.

GOAL: Check out your to-do list or notes and check off something on it today by actually doing it.

Day Thirteen: January 13

People often say motivation doesn't last. Well, neither does bathing—that's why we recommend it daily.

– Zig Ziglar

Have you ever felt pumped while reading a motivational quote? It's like you would go out there and put the world beneath your feet. Well, you might not feel like that anymore after a while. You need to say motivating words to yourself repeatedly. Staying strong isn't by being unsure; it is by making sure you get to the point where nothing can change your resolve about not giving up.

GOAL: Write down quotes that make you feel motivated the most and start taking them everywhere you go. Set your mobile phone alarm with amazing positive words to play a few times during your day.

Day Fourteen: January 14

Communicating with others helps you solve more problems.

Everyone is unique in their own way, and since no two people are perfectly alike, there could be disagreements. There is a way I see the world around me, which might not be the same way others see it. But I have come to understand that the basis of human relationship does not agree on everything, instead understanding helps to move past disagreements.

GOAL: Try to forgive and never stay mad at anyone for too long, if someone has offended you, try to talk to them about it. Explain how you felt and what they should do to avoid such occurrences.

Day Fifteen: January 15

Your imagination is your preview of life's coming attraction.

– Albert Einstein

Your mind is one of the best places to conceive dreams and create ideas. Start from the place of your mind and with strength, patience, and hard work, watch your dreams blossom into reality.

GOAL: Go over your imagination's limit and create mental images of where you want to be, and work toward it.

Day Sixteen: January 16

It always seems impossible until it is done.

– Nelson Mandela

I love one quote that says, "There is nothing like impossible, even the word in itself says I'm possible." The cell phone would have been termed impossible some 300 years ago, but it is now one of the best means of communication in this century. Don't ever think of anything as impossible, no matter how difficult it may seem. It only needs time, the right amount of effort and resource, and it will get done.

GOAL: Think about the tasks you have thought to be impossible, create possibilities by being positive, and work on them.

Day Seventeen: January 17

What you resist, persists.

– Carl Jung

Some things are necessary, and the more you try to push them forward, the more of an enigma they become. So why not take care of those things today and stop the procrastination.

GOAL: Believe that you can do anything as long as you put your mind to it. The time is now!

Day Eighteen: January 18

You are the best version of you.

The holy book says, "You are beautifully and wonderfully made," and it's high time you start believing that. There is only one you that has all the characteristics that you possess. No one can smile, laugh, or smirk the way you do. Even the sequence of your DNA is unique to only you. So stop the comparison, you are the most beautiful, wonderful, and best version of yourself.

GOAL: Anytime you see someone who you think is better or more beautiful than you, look back at "you are beautifully and wonderfully made" and find comfort in believing it.

Day Nineteen: January 19

Your worth consists in what you are and not what you have.

– Thomas Edison

Wealth, position, and riches do not make anyone better than who you are. Your definition of self-worth shouldn't be in how much money you have. Instead, it should be in your uniqueness and how you influence those around you and what you have to offer. I've been through times where I had nothing, but I came through by making sure my esteem never dropped. The world can throw a lot at you but get through each day by believing you are worth more than your circumstances.

GOAL: Are you passing through some derailing conditions? Always remember that you are who you are not because of circumstances, but who you choose to make yourself.

Day Twenty: January 20

Life is beauty, admire it.

– Mother Theresa

The world around is beautiful. Every time I go to the park or take a hike, the definition of the skyline, the horizon, and perfect greens that line the landscape is breathtaking. You just have to see beyond the heartaches, pain, and hurt and you would see it too.

GOAL: Go out today and experience the beauty of nature. Just empty your heart of all your worries and look beyond the chaos. Remember to take a deep breath and feel the inner peace.

Day Twenty-One: January 21

Through difficult experiences, life sometimes becomes more meaningful.

– Dalai Lama

Some of the greatest challenges I passed through has taught me the most important lesson. They have taught me patience, perseverance, and humility. It's not every day they come, but when they do, know that you have what it takes to get through it.

GOAL: Think about some of the most difficult situations that you have faced in life and how you overcame them. Pick out the lesson you learned.

Day Twenty-Two: January 22

Your potentials are limitless.

There is no limit to what we can achieve as humans; the only restriction we sometimes have is passion. Don't ever limit yourself, and it's up to you to make the best out of your life.

GOAL: Always believe you can do it with hard working and persistence. Remember that you can achieve anything.

Day Twenty-Three: January 23

Rock bottom became the solid foundation on which I rebuilt my life.

– J.K. Rowling

When things started falling from bad to worse for me, I thought I would never get back on my feet. But when I discovered that when you hit rock bottom, there is nowhere else to go but up. I started to build myself back from scratch. Making progress with each day, even though it was slow, I certainly got back to better days and eventually back on my two feet.

GOAL: No matter how bad it all gets, never give up. Remember the only way to go is up, especially when you hit rock bottom.

Day Twenty-Four: January 24

Behind every successful man, there's a lot of unsuccessful years.

– Bob Brown

The road to success is not smooth; neither is it easy. You would encounter a lot of hardship while trying to be successful. Try never to get discouraged. Just focus on your destination and keep pushing on.

GOAL: Write what you want to achieve and paste it somewhere you can see it every day. Let it motivate you to keep doing more.

Day Twenty-Five: January 25

Keep working to improve yourself.

There is no better way to give the best to the world around you than working on yourself first. So try to make sure you learn something new each day. Don't go to bed without becoming better at something, no matter how little it is.

GOAL: Work at something every day, no matter how little it is. Remember, little drops off water make a mighty ocean.

Day Twenty-Six: January 26

Your company defines you.

Long ago, I learned that I could never be better than the company I keep. Some part of me would always want to belong to my friends, family, and colleagues. If I am always around people who are bitter and negative, very soon, I would be a person who is also bitter and cynical. When I realized this, I immediately cut some people off. Not out of cruelty, but because I would never be able to be my best self when I'm around them.

GOAL: Get a notebook and write down the values you want to see in those people that surround you.

Day Twenty-Seven: January 27

Never let your past decisions determine your future outcome.

– Mark Dudley

Everyone is allowed to make mistakes, but don't let that define you. Every day is an opportunity to do something new and correct the errors of yesterday. Leave yesterday in the past and define your future.

GOAL: Don't let the mistake you made before weigh you down. Let go of the past and enjoy the present at the fullest.

Day Twenty-Eight: January 28

Every great person educates themselves.

– Nas

Truly great people have taught themselves how to be who they are, with self-discipline. What I learnt in school and what I learnt throughout from others were only enough to get me through a few things in life. I have come to understand that what I learnt through experience are what stuck best; they have taught me to be flexible and gave me the ability to cope and deal with several circumstances.

GOAL: Decide to educate yourself more today. How about doing an online course or starting that new language classes you have been dreaming of learning?

Day Twenty-Nine: January 29

Faith it, till you make it.

There have been so many times in life when all hope seems lost, and nothing seems to be in your favor. Trust me I have been there, what would get you through such times is faith. Believe in it even though you cannot see. As they say, your inner convictions would give you the energy to do more. I know as long as I have faith, I can push through any hardship or hopeless situations.

GOAL: Remember the times when it seems like you won't make it till the next day, and how you are still here. Stay strong!

Day Thirty: January 30

It's not the daily increase but the daily decrease. Hack away at the unessential.

–Bruce Lee

At first, this quote didn't make a lot of sense to me, not until I started to discover the fastest way to grow is to remove all the obstacles of growth. Don't just think about adding new things every day, instead look for the things that have hindered you from getting the best out of life. It could be a habit or friends. Just take a look at all the things you would be better off without.

GOAL: List down all negatives, dramas, and toxic people in your life and start working to remove one each day.

Day Thirty-One: January 31

We all need somebody to lean on.

– Bill Withers

When push comes to shove, and all the chips are down, we come to realize that we are not in this alone. As much as I have come to rely on my inner strength, I have also come to realize that we need someone to share life with. It is easy to become depressed when all emotions are internalized. So stop isolating yourself and get connected to those around you. Have someone to share your best moments and mourn the sad ones.

GOAL: Start learning how to seek support from others, go out of your way and rebuild all the relationships you have left in the past.

FEBRUARY

Day Thirty-Two: February 1

Never be too shy to stand out.

You don't need to try too hard to fit in, sometimes it's better to stand out. There is no one who doesn't have unique abilities, so don't allow the crowd to suck you in. Stand up for yourself and let the world around you feel how beautiful your potentials are.

GOAL: No matter your eccentricities, don't try to hide them. Let the world see you for who you are and embrace you.

Day Thirty-Three: February 2

Failure will never overtake me if my determination to succeed is strong enough.

– Og Mandino

You would encounter several things in this life that would knock the wind out of you. They are bound to happen, but your mindset would determine if they keep you down or make you stronger. I have learned how to see every challenge as an opportunity to get better at facing the difficulties life brings. The key is to draw on your inner strength and refuse to back down.

GOAL: No matter what you are going through, have a firm resolve never to let it be the end of you but to make a new you!

Day Thirty-Four: February 3

Be the change you wish to see in the world.

– Mahatma Gandhi

The best way to influence people is to become what you want to see them. Nothing works likes leading by example, and this is something that applies when it comes to change. The more you change, the more you see the change that you desire to see.

GOAL: Make a list of all the things that you would love to see others do and decide to do it first. Beautiful things are going to happen.

Day Thirty-Five: February 4

Your time is limited, so don't waste it living someone else's life.

–Steve Jobs

It's so easy to get carried away by how others are living, and this can make us lose track of ourselves for a while. But look at the world, someone once said "no one is going to get out of this life alive." So why waste time sulking about the things that you could have had. Go out, take a walk, take a day off and relax, go to the park and have ice cream, do something that you haven't done for a while and remember to have fun while at it.

GOAL: Take out a day to go out to have fun, select different activities, and do something for yourself, it can be a spa or something you used to do a long time ago.

Day Thirty-Six: February 5

Remember you're the one who can fill the world with sunshine.

– Snow White

Disney has always had words of wisdom between the lines of their animation. Take your dose of sunshine and add it to the word every morning. Feelings can be transferred, so don't transfer your pain, anger, or hurt. Instead, be part of creating a world filled with sunshine and joy.

GOAL: Whatever worries you have, try to resolve within yourself and never to let it affect how you behave to others. Practice that smile in the mirror and go out to reflect happiness.

Day Thirty-Seven: February 6

Live truthfully, and you would have lived a better life.

What I have come to appreciate about life is that it's never just a pure emotion; it's always a roller coaster of feelings that keep everything alive. Love, anxiety, sadness, they could all come at once, you don't need to learn to control all of them at a time. Learn every day that life is a texture of feelings, and the only way to experience true beauty is to be truthful to yourself in every moment.

GOAL: If you have a mix of feelings, try to talk to a friend or book an appointment with a professional who will guide you to the best way to release your thoughts and emotions. Meditation also helps loads.

Day Thirty-Eight: February 7

The energy of the mind is the essence of life.

–Aristotle

Motivational quotes and speeches have always been around me, but I never got them to work for me until I realized that it was a thing of the mind. No matter how much you read these quotes and words of encouragement, they would only work to the extent to which you apply your mind to it. Channel your energy into building your mind and your life would have more essence and meaning.

GOAL: Decide not only to read these quotes every day but also to make sure you apply them to your life.

Day Thirty-Nine: February 8

Sometimes it's okay to step back and think only about yourself.

In life, you cannot save others before saving yourself. Sometimes it may seem selfish to consider only yourself but think about it. You wouldn't be able to help others if you are not well. Take a day off, eat that last piece of pizza, do something to make sure that you are healthy and strong enough to give your best to others. It's all about balancing it well enough to have the best of yourself while serving others.

GOAL: Try to take care of yourself today. Get a foot rub, go to the cinema, or sleep in.

Day Forty: February 9

Prepare to win the night before.

– Les Brown

If you check out the story of the most successful people, you will find out that there are no accidents. They got where they are today not by wishing and sitting on their asses. No, they had a plan, and they followed it. Sometimes what stops us from achieving our true potential is the amount of strategy and hard work we are willing to put into our dreams.

GOAL: Get a notepad and start a blueprint to where you want to be in years to come. Make your plans achievable and time-dependent.

Day Forty-One: February 10

I'm tough, I'm ambitious, and I know exactly what I want.

– Madonna

The quote might seem a little harsh, but in life, you can never please everyone. In getting to where you want to be, you must be ready to step on people's toes and face criticism. Remember, however, that the world doesn't always want what is best for you. People are generally more comfortable with being on the same level as you. So when you start moving forward, they don't like the idea of being left behind. But you have just got to do what is best for you.

GOAL: Decide to move forward and never look back, no matter who tries to drag you down.

Day Forty-Two: February 11

You have only one life; if it is not going in the direction you want, now is the time to change.

– Joyce Meyer

The truth about death is that it is inevitable for everyone. Each passing day brings us closer and closer to this reality. The realization if this helps you keep a check on your life. So if you have a job, life, or relationship that is not working the way you would like to. There is no better time to stir it in the right direction than now.

GOAL: Decide to work on everything that isn't working right in your life and open your path to good vibrations.

Day Forty-Three: February 12

Life without purpose is meaningless.

– Amy Torres

Imagine how boring life would be if you wake up each morning without having anything to do. That is why everyone has a purpose, and there is a particular purpose you are meant to meet each single day. You can discover your purpose by looking for what you enjoy doing. When I found mine, it totally changed my outlook on life. I started enjoying what I do more, and there wasn't a scarcity of passion.

GOAL: List everything you love doing and try to define your purpose from it. You can also get books on how to discover your purpose and work toward it.

Day Forty-Four: February 13

I can never be safe, always try and go against the grain. As soon as I accomplish one thing, I just set a higher goal. That is how I have gotten to where I am.

– Beyoncé

Immediately I got back on my two feet. I started to get comfortable with where I am, and then I saw this quote. It's never enough to be good when there is better and best. This made me decide not only to stand but to walk, run, and eventually fly.

GOAL: Push yourself to leave your comfort zone and do something more as from today.

Day Forty-Five: February 14

Your mind, body, and soul are your greatest assets. Take care of them.

Three essential components make up every human, and that is the mind, the body, and the soul. And the key to living a healthy life is to take care of the three of them. Be your own critic, love yourself, and treat yourself with as much kindness as you can give. It's a big part of your journey to loving yourself.

GOAL: Every morning when you wake up, add it to your routine to appreciate how beautiful you are, both inside and out. Look in the mirror and see how blessed you are!

Day Forty-Six: February 15

Sometimes when opportunities don't come knocking, go out and grab them.

You don't always have to wait for an opportunity to come crawling down your path, you should be determined to go out of your way to create one. There are opportunities everywhere, but you won't find them where you are, you have to break protocols and defy the norm to get them.

GOAL: Explore the opportunities around you, be in contact with your networking, check some online groups which are talking about the same subject you are interested in, be creative, and believe in yourself.

Day Forty-Seven: February 16

Black or white, no race is better than any other race.

No matter your race or ethnicity, it doesn't really matter. You are not defined by your background. We are all equal and have the same shot at greatness. Never let anyone get your spirit down with their myopic view.

GOAL: Try to see everyone as being equal and educate others too. We are the same, we are one.

Day Forty-Eight: February 17

You are the only one that has the power to change your life, others can only try or teach you the path to follow.

Starting the journey to success is not something that anyone can do for you. Even if you have studied courses or have a guide who teaches you the ropes, it is your own personal decision to either follow the instructions or leave them rotting in your library of knowledge. The main thing is to get yourself to start acting out all that you have learned and work with them toward your goal.

GOAL: The determination to achieve your goal lies within you and only you have the power to activate it.

Day Forty-Nine: February 18

The night is never too old and the day is never too young.

I thought of this quote while having a very bad day, things kept turning out the way I didn't want them to and it was getting frustrating. That's when I caught a wisp of *The Night Is Still Young* by Nicki Minaj. And then I thought, it's never too late to start the day all over again. So I found somewhere to meditate and kind of reset. The whole process causes my mood to reset and gets me back on the drive for the day.

GOAL: When your day is going rough, think about happy memories, like the time things were really going smoothly and live in those moments for a while; it would get your mood up and change your perspective.

Day Fifty: February 19

If you do the work, you get rewarded, there are no shortcuts in life.

– Michael Jordan

One thing that you have to believe about life is that there are no handouts. If you want something, you have to go out, work hard, and get it. There is no easy way to become the person you have always admired and wished you were.

GOAL: Start working on your dreams today, not only wishing them.

Day Fifty-One: February 20

I'm so blessed to have so many great things in my life – family, friends and God.

– Lil' Kim

Sometimes when I'm feeling down or distraught, what gets me back to the happy place is remembering everything I have. Looking at the missing section of the cake would not make you feel better, but see it from the perspective of everything you possess. You have a lot to be thankful for, your family, your friends, and God. Stop living in misery and start enjoying what you have been blessed with.

GOAL: Anytime you start feeling like you don't have enough, take a jotter and list all you have achieved.

Day Fifty-Two: February 21

Let us always meet each other with a smile, for the smile is the beginning of love.

– Mother Theresa

The effect of a genuine smile can make someone's day. I have never represented who I am to others more confidently with when I am met with a good smile. There is something it does to my exuberance that cannot be explained. When I'm meeting people, I try to give them my most genuine smile and help to be part of the beauty that lights up their world.

GOAL: Anytime you are meeting up with someone, give them your most genuine smile not only with your mouth but with your eyes too.

Day Fifty-Three: February 22

No matter how small you start, always dream big.

– Stephen Richards

The most important thing is not about how you start, it's about how big you grow. And you never grow by been short-sighted. You should always dream big, no matter how small your project seems now. Look at the future and see something so big it appears crazy; only then you would grow.

GOAL: Whatever you are doing, always have the goal of growing big. Use what you have, your resources, to do something meaningful today.

Day Fifty-Four: February 23

Don't just exist, live.

Everything can get so stressful at times and you start to move with the flow. But it's better to stop and look around. Are you really living or just existing? Never lose your essence in the struggles live throws at you.

GOAL: Focus on enjoying life, instead of just letting life knock you about. Do something that makes you feel good today, call someone you miss and have a nice chat.

Day Fifty-Five: February 24

Everything you've ever wanted is on the other side of fear.

– George Addair

Fear is one of the things that would keep you in your cage and stunt your growth. You have to know that overcoming your fear is the pathway to true freedom. Remember, fear is not irrational but it is irrational if you allow fear to get the best of you.

GOAL: Rise above any obstacles placed in your way so that you become the person that you really are. Be brave!

Day Fifty-Six: February 25

Loneliness and the feeling of being unwanted is the most terrible poverty.

– Mother Teresa

No matter the position or status you are at in life, they would not make you feel loved the way people would. It is natural for everyone to desire that feeling of being cared for and nurtured from another person. And nothing brings this feeling better than those that surround you.

GOAL: Do something special for someone close to you. Be more conscious of spreading love and happiness.

Day Fifty-Seven: February 26

When you know what you want, and want it bad enough, you'll find a way to get it.

– *Jim Rohn*

Have you ever been so hungry that you thought to yourself, "I would do anything for a chocolate right now?" We have all been in that place where a certain craving becomes so strong we could not but satisfy it. That is how you craving for success should be the big picture in your mind every day and dwell on it till it becomes the very force that drives you.

GOAL: Think about where you want to be in the nearest future. Do this through the day until you have it all mapped out in your head and write it down.

Day Fifty-Eight: February 27

Our imperfections are what makes us perfect.

No one is perfect, I know you must have heard this phrase several times. But you have to start believing it is true. We aren't perfect, so when we make mistakes or do something wrong, try not to dwell on it all day. Look back, learn from it, and move on.

GOAL: If there is any mistake that you have made and it's weighing you down, shake it off and remember it's in the past, just look into the future.

Day Fifty-Nine: February 28

Do what you can with all you have, wherever you are.

– Theodore Roosevelt

It's important to give all you can, no matter where you are. Never limit yourself to the resources available, instead open your mind to the possibilities you can create with what is available. I learned something long ago, that I can do anything with nothing, all I have to do is to be ready to think out of the box.

GOAL: Look around you and start thinking about the several possibilities that you can make happen with those things and the people you know.

MARCH

Day Sixty: March 1

Start each day with a positive thought and a grateful heart.

– Roy T. Bennett

Each day is a chance to do something new, and it is a fresh start, a beautiful opening of a new chapter in your life. Just think about how great it is to be alive to see another sun coming up on the horizon. This alone should make you wake up with a grateful heart and think positive things about the day. Don't let the sorrows of yesterday weigh you down, be determined to forge ahead and make something of this beautiful new beginning.

GOAL: Look outside and appreciate the beauty of the day, then pen down all the positive things you would like to achieve today.

Day Sixty-One: March 2

Mix a little foolishness with your serious plans; it's lovely to be silly at the right moment.

– Horace

In life, being serious all the time would cause you heartaches that aren't necessary. You have to realize that, most of the time, things are not too serious. Try to enjoy what you do more, throw in a little joke in your conversation, laugh freely, and don't forget to breathe.

GOAL: Put on a comedy tape and have a few laughs before stepping out this morning.

Day Sixty-Two: March 3

You can choose not to let your condition get the better of you.

It would have been effortless for me to allow everything that happens in my life get the better of me, but that wouldn't have helped me or anyone reading this book. You can choose to stay down and let your challenges walk all over you, or you can choose to stand up and make your experience become a lesson to you and others who would read your story too.

GOAL: Think about a situation you are going through and look for a way to turn it into something inspirational.

Day Sixty-Three: March 4

Life is much more fun if you love it in the spirit of play and collaboration, working with, instead of against, others.

– *Wally Amos*

Always treat other people with the same kindness that you treat yourself. You never know what tomorrow could bring for them. The janitor at your workplace today can be the first to get to your scene of help and wouldn't it be funny how the tables would now turn. So never get too cocky in life, no one needs that. Be kind to everyone, regardless of their status and positions.

GOAL: Always let your positive attitude and words uplift the souls of who you meet.

Day Sixty-Four: March 5

Surround yourself with the people that bring out the best in you.

There is no better way to grow than surrounding yourself with people that make you the best version of yourself. Over the years, people around me have been instrumental to my success; they have shaped, motivated, and inspired me to be more than I am each day.

GOAL: Look around you and list what positive things people around you have done in your development. If you can find none, it's time to start surrounding yourself with new people.

Day Sixty-Five: March 6

Don't feel stupid if you don't like what everyone else pretends to love.

– Emma Watson

Have you ever felt odd simply because you didn't like what everyone else seems to be falling head over heels for? Well, what you need to question is your feeling wrong about having a different opinion. Someone once said wrong is wrong, no matter how many people think it's right. You don't need to like something and never pretend you do.

GOAL: Don't pretend to like something; no rule book says you must accept something simply because everyone loves it. Just live in harmony but keep distance from who do not add anything to you.

Day Sixty-Six: March 7

Above all else, guard your heart, for everything you do flows from it.

The holy book is full of wisdom, and this verse from it makes a remarkable quote. You have to be careful about the information you let seep into your mind. Your mind won't merely store this information, keep reading as it brings you calm and peace and perhaps to find words for what you already know. So try as much as possible to have as many positive thoughts as possible.

GOAL: Start each day with positive thoughts and go over the quotes you read over and over again. Meditate on them every hour.

Day Sixty-Seven: March 8

Every child is an artist. The problem is how to remain an artist once he grows up.

– *Pablo Picasso*

Your sense of wonder, innocence, and freedom are the most excellent tool for creativity, but most often, we lose all of them as we grow up. The struggles of work, bills, and everything about adulthood suppresses them. However, you have to stay determined, never to lose yourself completely, appreciate the world around you, and with a masterstroke, use these tools to shape who you are and who you are becoming.

GOAL: Create time for your hobby and do the things you loved while growing up. Never be too busy to have fun.

Day Sixty-Eight: March 9

Change is good.

– Rafiki (Lion king)

Change is one of the worst nightmares of several people, but without change, there can be no progress. I have had to change a lot of things in my life. From jobs to home and more, change is constant. It can be slow, and the process can be painful, but in the end, good change brings about progress. "Remember, tough situations don't last, only tough people do."

GOAL: Have you been stalling on something because you don't want a change? Now is the time to start the process. Believe that many good things are coming!

Day Sixty-Nine: March 10

You define your own story; you write your chapters in this book called life.

A lot has happened to me these past few years, and when I look back at each situation, they were part of what got me to where I am now. Life has thought me that it doesn't have to be a book of misery. You can make the best use of each new chapter and rewrite your future into an amazing one. Don't be discouraged when things start going south; instead, look up and decide that it is the only place worth going to.

GOAL: Never let your present circumstances discourage you, get back up, and start striving to move forward. Write down your dreams and plans for the near future.

Day Seventy: March 11

Define your style.

When it comes to style, you have the freedom to choose your own. You can choose to be simple, modern, or add layers of colors to accentuate your beauty. Just make sure it is something that you love and would make you look amazing.

GOAL: Whenever picking out your dress today, be unique. You can do something you have always wanted to do and be sure it is appropriate for your outing.

Day Seventy-One: March 12

Smile and let everyone know that today, you're a lot stronger than you were yesterday.

– Drake

A smile is the reflection of the heart's state. Put on your best smile today, as you move along the walk or around your office or home.

GOAL: Smile all through the day, no matter what happens. Smile at yourself in the mirror and see what a beautiful soul you are!

Day Seventy-Two: March 13

Either do not begin or having begun, do not give up.

– Chinese Proverb

It is not starting something that matters; it is making sure that you see it till the end. Be motivated and drive yourself to finish anything that you have begun. And it doesn't matter how slow or fast you go. What matters is that you keep going until it is complete.

GOAL: If there is any goal you started and have not completed, stop procrastinating, and start working on it today. Make it happen, life is NOW!

Day Seventy-Three: March 14

Never give up your dreams, not for anything in the world.

Your ideas and vision are the keys to creating your future, and you should never let them go. It may seem like they would never come through, and it is time to face reality, but don't make that happen. Look at the future and always see the possibilities of doing that one thing that you have always held in your heart. At least, you would have no regrets even if it doesn't work out, because you would know you tried.

GOAL: If you have written down specific visions and dreams or you have some embedded in your mind, now is the time to start working on it. Make a check list for it.

Day Seventy-Four: March 15

The world would be a better place if you play your part and I play mine.

I have always been a believer that the world would be better for generations to come, and I don't just sit and wait for it to happen, I do something about it. I have served in different volunteer organizations over the years and help to do things like; tending to the orphanage, making donations to charities that cater for the less privileged, and engaging in community services. If I do my own little and you do your own little, soon all our little would come together and make a significant impact on the world.

GOAL: Look for a cause that you are passionate about and volunteer for it. Check on the internet the organizations around your city that you can join to this amazing cause.

Day Seventy-Five: March 16

It is a mistake to look too far ahead. The chain of destiny can only be grasped one link at a time.

– Winston Churchill

It is often good to place a lot of importance on getting something you have always wanted or achieving your dreams. But never be too much in a hurry that you get carried away by the process. Success is not achieved overnight, so why not cool it and slow down. Take one step after the other, not one leap after the other. The aim is to look at and think about the final destination and let the journey take its course.

GOAL: Have you been in a hurry to get something? Sit down today and think about the end, then decide not to get carried away.

Day Seventy-Six: March 17

Our lives begin to end, the day we become silent over things that matter.

–Martin Luther King Jr.

Standing up for something is the true essence of humanity. You have to learn to be bold and make a stand for the thing that matters. The truth is, there might be someone, somewhere waiting for someone to take the lead. But they would never know if you cower and let fear get the best of you.

GOAL: Never be too scared to stand up for the things you believe in, you might be making the world a better place by letting your stand known. And you would sleep better knowing you have done your best.

Day Seventy-Seven: March 18

The meaning of life is to find your gift. The purpose of life is to give it away.

– *William Shakespeare*

There is more to life than just your happiness, and thinking about yourself alone won't cut it. Try to do something that makes others find happiness. Whatever you gift is, it can be used for serving the greater good of humanity.

GOAL: Use your gift and talents to serve the humanity.

Day Seventy-Eight: March 19

Count your blessings.

The hymn says, "count your blessings name them one by one." This is a very good strategy to live every day with a feeling of happiness. You don't have to look at the things you don't have and feel sad, what you have is good enough. Don't be a half-empty bottle person, instead be the type that sees the bottle half full.

GOAL: Look around you and be grateful for the things you do have, no matter how little they are. I'm sure you will find out how much blessed you are.

Day Seventy-Nine: March 20

Being contented leads to happiness, but complacency leads to future misery.

Life is all about finding that perfect balance, so while you are in a happy place with what you have, you don't have to sit there. You need to keep moving forward. The right balance is, never be too jealous or over-zealous to get there, but move steadily and surely while making sure that you are happy through the process.

GOAL: Be happy with things you have now, and enjoy them while you move forward to achieve even more.

Day Eighty: March 21

Life is not a spectator sport, if watching is all you are gonna do, then you are gonna watch your life go by without ya.

– Quasimodo (The Hunchback of Notre Dame)

Don't just sit by and watch life go by, go out and experience it. This is the lesson behind the story of the hunchback of Notre dame portrayed by Disney. Don't be too comfortable with things happening around you and then going by without you experiencing them. Don't miss someone's birthday, take that girl you like out, talk to the guy you admire, leave every day enjoying the joy and pain it brings.

GOAL: Dare to do something rare today. Make your day even more special!

Day Eighty-One: March 22

Live as if your prayers are to be answered.

– Anonymous

Being optimistic about life is a great asset to possess. You can live every day with the faith that everything you ask for is happening. I had seen things happen when I believed they could, and this alone is remarkable enough to make me wake up in the morning and ask for the things I want the day to bring me, and I go believing I'll have it before the day ends.

GOAL: Ask for what you want the day/month/year to bring you and live like you have it. Even if it doesn't work every single time quickly, it helps you keep an optimistic attitude.

Day Eighty-Two: March 23

I ask not for a lighter burden but for a broader shoulder.

– Proverb

There was a time I always wished everything would go easy on me, I wished my job would be easy, and I would get more money; instead, things got harder. That's when I learned that building my capacity to do more is actually better than waiting for things to get easier. Work smart, not so hard.

GOAL: Try to build your capacity to do more today instead of waiting for things to get easy. You are more strong than you can imagine.

Day Eighty-Three: March 24

The darkest nights always lead to the brightest dawn.

When things get really tough, be assured that they can only get better. Terrible situations are usually a prelude for the best that is yet to come. Sometimes all you have to do is brave the darkness, and you would soon find the brightest of light.

GOAL: Never give up, no matter how bad it becomes. Be patient and trust the process of it.

Day Eighty-Four: March 25

A big part of being a well-adjusted person is accepting that you can't be good at everything.

– Kelly Williams Brown

Something that I have learned over the years is to embrace my gifts and not be jealous of others who excel in something else. You certainly can't be good at everything. You can excel at counting numbers while someone else is awesome when it comes to strings and numbers. But the key to happiness is to embrace what you are good at and make the best of it.

GOAL: Have you been trying to go out of your way to learn something because somebody else is good at it? Stop it and embrace your won gifts. Valuing yourself is the best thing you can do.

Day Eighty-Five: March 26

Plan a day that makes you jump out of bed in the morning.

– Anonymous

Motivation is built by continuous meditation. You can plan a day that literally gets you racing out of bed in the morning. Before you get a shut-eye at night, plan your next day, dream big, and never limit your imagination to the resources available.

GOAL: Try this, imagine a day that is filled with potential, and motivate yourself toward it before you sleep at night.

Day Eighty-Six: March 27

The best way to live is to live forever young.

The more you grow, the more the world also changes. To keep adapting to these changes, you need to learn how to stay forever young. This doesn't mean being a physical youth, and it means that you have to keep learning and be ready to accept the changes that come with it.

GOAL: Never be hesitant to learn something new each day. You can do anything by any age. You're great and smart just the way you are.

Day Eighty-Seven: March 28

Weeping may endure for a night but joy cometh in the morning.

Tears are seen as a sign of weakness, so a lot of us hold it in. The more you do that, the more you allow it to tear you apart. It's okay to let the tears sometimes flow because what comes after is a lighter heart, ready to face the battle with renewed vigor. Don't worry, after the tears comes something amazing.

GOAL: It's okay to let those tears flow, as long as you remember that there would be joy after.

Day Eighty-Eight: March 29

Believe deep down in your heart that you are destined to do great things. – Joe Paterno

I have lived through various ups and downs in my life, and some of them made it so hard to believe that things would be good again truly. But now, after so many stormy clouds and the sun shining through, I can now see that they were setting me up for something greater. Life can get very tough, but we are never meant to remain in that bad place for too long.

GOAL: Never believe that you are destined to remain in bad times; there is something more. You are more than just a particle in the ocean, and you best start believing that.

Day Eighty-Nine: March 30

No matter how talented you are, not everybody is going to like you. But that's life, just stay strong.

– *Justin Bieber*

In life, not everyone is going to like you, no matter how good or bad you are. It doesn't matter if you woke up one day and distributed all your money to those around you; someone would still not like you. So don't live to please everybody, just be the best you can be and stay strong for criticism that might follow.

GOAL: There would always be people who would criticize you, never let them get to you. Stay strong, walk tall, and keep striving to be better.

Day Ninety: March 31

Follow your heart.

Believing in what your heart tells you to do is very important most times. There are a lot of places where you could get directions, your head, your heart, and your friends would try to help you see the best way to go. But the truth is that all routes can't be right. Make sure you think deeply and listen to the wise whispers of your heart before taking a final decision.

GOAL: Choose wisely next time you decide to do something; listen to and follow your heart.

APRIL

Day Ninety-One: April 1

To lead with excellence, you must have the right attitude. Excellence is a quality of a person's right attitude about how they do things.

– Brian Cagneey

The right attitude is essential when it comes to excellence. You have to have the right mindset and make sure that you do things the right way.

GOAL: Anytime you find yourself in a position of leadership, make sure you do it with an excellent mindset and fully from your heart.

Day Ninety-Two: April 2

Peace comes from the mind, do not seek it without.

– Buddha

Have you ever had everything around you falling to chaos and it seemed like you were never going to get out unscathed? Well, if you are reading this, then it means you are still alive. In life, inner peace is the most essential thing that you can have. I have learned how to remain calm in stormy situations because the situation would certainly pass, and I would be left with whatever damage I allowed it to do to me.

GOAL: If you are you going through a rough patch, try to calm your nerves, and find that inner peace. Reassure yourself that all would be well until you believe it. Remind yourself of something you went through in the past and overcame it.

Day Ninety-Three: April 3

Discipline with passion is the key to greatness.

Passion is great and would push you to love what you do, but you need discipline to be truly great. Those that have achieved greatness have displayed dexterity along with discipline. So it's not just about the love, it's the ability to do those things even when you don't have any inspiration to. Trust me, it's not every day you are going to wake up feeling like picking up your guitar to practice, or standing up and counting numbers for yet another day. But discipline is the driving force for days like this.

GOAL: Make sure you do whatever it takes to keep doing what you love, even when you don't feel like doing it. Have a nice shower, dress up, and remember how special and amazing you are.

Day Ninety-Four: April 4

Ice melts into rain, love turns into pain. Here I go again, falling in love again.

– Wale

Live is full of heartbreaks and hurt is not far away from the loving heart, but you can choose not to let it stop your heart from living every day filled with love. Whatever you do, let your heart fall in love again and again. Don't let seeing the sunrise get too old, appreciate the beauty of the daffodils, and the lovely scent of your colleague's perfume. Let your day be filled with wonder, and your heart would be filled with joy.

GOAL: Love every day and all that comes with every single one. Love brings us peace, especially within our self-love.

Day Ninety-Five: April 5

We have two lives and the second begins when we realize we have one.

– Confucius

Understanding that we have one life might can be the best thing we ever discover. When I think and remember that I wouldn't live twice, it helps me make bold decisions and do things that I would otherwise not have done.

GOAL: Take that bold step today, you might not have another chance to do it. Show your attitude and rock like a star.

Day Ninety-Six: April 6

Keep moving, no matter how difficult the journey gets.

You would have heard several times how life is not a bed of roses, well, it's true. You cannot expect to have an easy path to success. Else everyone would be successful. So no matter what you are going through now, just know that it is one of the necessary experiences to get to your destination.

GOAL: When you seem to be experiencing a chaos, always think about the good destination you are heading to. You eventually get to the best place as you deserve to.

Day Ninety-Seven: April 7

We all have to take defeats.

– Muhammad Ali

I have had a lot of challenges in my life that didn't go away as soon as I wanted them to. But a friend of mine kept telling me of how life teaches you how to take defeats to prepare you for what is ahead. And it made sense; life is a teacher, and some of its lessons might not be so pleasant, but just like in school, we must learn to take the failure and build them into reaping the success.

GOAL: Beautiful soul: You are made to do hard things so believe in yourself. Transform, feel, and live it.

Day Ninety-Eight: April 8

Focused will is incredible.

– Yanni

There is nothing like having your will channeled in the right direction. There would be no stopping you as you barrel your way into greatness.

GOAL: Place your focus and follow through. Always focus on the good.

Day Ninety-Nine: April 9

Remember: Every champion was once a contender who refused to give up.

– Rocky Balboa

If you have a dream, but things aren't working out, then try to look for people who have gone ahead and done something similar. They have won some of the battles you are fighting and can guide you through them. My mentor was really helpful when I faced problems and situations that seemed to be way out of my league. But through guidance and mentorship, I was able to come out on the other side with lessons learned, and battles won.

GOAL: Look for someone who has gone through what you are going through and try to seek their advice. Remember that we are all in the same boat with different and similar directions.

Day One-Hundred: April 10

When people treat you like nothing, you begin to feel like nothing.

– *Drake*

Never let anyone define how you feel. I have been mocked several times by people who ended up on the sidelines appreciating my achievements. So leave out the outside opinions, especially when it is interfering with your dreams.

GOAL: Never let people define your feelings; you are who you make yourself. Stay surrounded by those who lift you up.

Day One-Hundred-and-One: April 11

Never let failure keep you down.

Don't ever think for a second that you wouldn't fail sometimes. Failure is part of life. It's one of the things that teach you that life is all rosy. What you can choose to do, however, is to determine if you would learn from it or allow it to keep you down. I have failed in life and trust me, it was not a good thing, but I have long learned to stand up each time I fail and get better at what I failed at.

GOAL: Is there anything you have failed doing? Get back on track and try to do it in another way. Learn from your mistakes and proceed.

Day One-Hundred-and-Two: April 12

Be a fountain, not a drain.

– *Rex Hudler*

Thinking about others is one thing that I have found fulfilling in my life. In this world, you are not the only one around, so you have to think of others. Make sure that you aren't just talking, do something for others. Go out of your way once in a while to show those around you that you appreciate them. Greet someone, make a new friend, and never forget to contribute your bit to the world around you.

GOAL: Do something for someone today and make them feel special.

Day One-Hundred-and-Three: April 13

Your value doesn't decrease by someone's inability to see your worth.

– Anonymous

Always remember these words when you get rejected or criticized by people. You aren't a failure or a train wreck because someone says you are. You are the only person that can define who you are. Neither your employer nor your colleagues should hold the key to your beliefs. Anything they think shouldn't get to you. You are bold, gorgeous, the best thing that happened to the world, let that be your drive every single day.

GOAL: Life is too short to worry about small things. Stay positive, it will take their breath way.

Day One-Hundred-and-Four: April 14

They're no such things as 'too late.'

As long as you are alive, there is always time for correction, always time to start again, or switch direction. Don't ever be deceived by age or time; I've realized that I am in control of my future by deciding how I spend mine now.

GOAL: If there is any good time to start that plan or project of your yours, the time is now.

Day One-Hundred-and-Five: April 15

It is easier to prevent bad habits than to break them.

– Benjamin Franklin

Bad habits don't have any advantage, and there is no reason to keep them. They would only end up stopping your growth. It's better to stop feeding that habit now before it spoils your whole plan and health.

GOAL: Make a checklist of all the habits that you have and start working on stopping the ones that are hindering your growth.

Day One-Hundred-and-Six: April 16

The gem cannot be polished without friction, nor man perfected without trails.

– *Chinese Proverb*

Every time I try to move a step ahead in life, I have to increase the amount of work I put into what I do. Through this, I have learned that getting better is not just about the philosophy, and you have to throw some hard work in there and break some more sweat than you are used to. You would definitely have to be in new terrain when trying out new things, but you will get better as you journey along.

GOAL: Get out of your comfort zone and try moving to the next level in your career or whatever you do.

Day One-Hundred-and-Seven: April 17

Work hard, stay positive, and get up early. It's the best part of the day.

– George Allen

Something I learned long ago about a day is that the earliest part is the best. Once you get past the general fatigue that is coming as you wake up, you can do a lot in those early hours. So, after a long day, try to get a shower, get into bed early, and wake up feeling positive and add some meditation or exercises to your early schedule.

GOAL: Make the best use of the early part of your day. Meditate, exercise, and motivate yourself.

Day One-Hundred-and-Eight: April 18

Be gentle with yourself, you are doing the best you can.

– Unknown

Quotes, motivational talks, and encouragement are all very good, but never try to push yourself too hard. The best thing is to find the perfect balance and give yourself a break once in a while.

GOAL: It's time to evaluate your progress, appreciate yourself, and just breathe.

Day One-Hundred-and-Nine: April 19

The most courageous act is still to think for yourself. Aloud.

– Coco Chanel

There is no limit to growing up, and it's something that we do every day. When I first got out of some of the challenges I was facing, I thought, this was it. Certainly, everything would start to fall into place now. But nothing could be as deceptive as this. I still had and have several obstacles to cross. From this, I have learned that every day is a new opportunity to think for myself, without being too scared to move forward and accept the challenges that my thoughts may bring.

GOAL: Trust your own intuition. Another's mind isn't walking your journey, but you.

Day One-Hundred-and-Ten: April 20

Find happiness in every day and never let it go.

Every day brings its dose of happiness and sadness, and you have a choice to make. You can go through it sulking and never seeing the things that can make you happy. Or you can be so happy, and nothing can get you sad. It's all in what you decide to choose.

GOAL: Find your inspiration for happiness every day and never let anything make you sad. Remember something that you are so happy about it.

Day One-Hundred-and-Eleven: April 21

To expect defeat is nine-tenths of defeat itself.

– Francis Crawford

Life works in an amazing way; the things you get are attracted by what you think and feel. So if you set out expecting defeat than you have to know that sooner or later you would get it. I once learned somewhere that the things you fear the most are masters over you. And it taught me that overcoming the fear of failure is a big part of overcoming failure.

GOAL: If you're feeling happy or sad, that too can color our interpretation of a situation. You are getting ready for the next level.

Day One-Hundred-and-Twelve: April 22

Regardless of how it goes down, life goes on.

– Rick Ross

The Earth hangs in the solar system and revolves around the Sun 24 hours a day and 365 days a year. It doesn't stop when someone dies or takes a break to celebrate someone's success. So why stop moving because you are facing some trials. No matter what happens, success or failure, keep on moving cause the world's never going to wait for you.

GOAL: Focusing on the gratitude. It's one of the most powerful human emotions; once expressed and felt, it changes attitude and broadens our perspective.

Day One-Hundred-and-Thirteen: April 23

An eye for an eye would only make the world blind.

– Mahatma Gandhi

I have had so many things done to me by people that seem unforgivable at the moment. But the thought of having to live with a burden that creates for my heart is not an option. There is a peace that comes with forgiveness, and I find it each time I let go of the wrongs others have done to me.

GOAL: Think about any grudge you are holding and let it go. Lift the weight off your shoulder and experience the inner peace that comes with letting go.

Day One-Hundred-and-Fourteen: April 24

Never be scared of mistakes, they only teach you how not to do something.

I started reading books, and they explained how mistakes are just an opportunity to learn something new. This information transformed me and helped me break the barriers I would have never dreamt of breaking before.

GOAL: Mistakes are not what stops greatness; it is failing to learn from them that do. Learn from your mistakes. Mostly importantly: forgive yourself.

Day One-Hundred-and-Fifteen: April 25

The things that make me different are the things that make me, me.

– Piglet (Winnie the Pooh)

You are different from every other person by those things that make you unique. Never lose yourself in the process of trying to become what people want you to. People would definitely want you to be the version of yourself they like, and while that is nice, it's not possible. Stay true to yourself and make your happiness a priority.

GOAL: You are unique, and no one should make you feel otherwise.

Day One-Hundred-and-Sixteen: April 26

Life is like a cup of tea, it's all in how you make it.

– Irish quote

Your future is being shaped by every single decision you are making now. It's just like the condiments you add into a soup; what you put into the pot would determine the kind of soup you are making. Devote your plans and decision to an outcome that would have good reflections on your future.

GOAL: Think about what you want your future to be like. Then start laying down plans and work toward it.

Day One-Hundred-and-Seventeen: April 27

Every human walks around with a certain kind of sadness. They may not wear it on their sleeves, but it's there if you look deep.

– Taraji P. Henson

Everyone has their battle that they are fighting and they might not even look like it. Try not to judge people by the way they act, and you should sometimes leave room for contingency. 'What of if the person just receives very disheartening news, or just lost something or someone precious to them.' The way people act is sometimes a reflection of what they are going through secretly. It's not every time you judge someone as bad because they acted out, who knows, they may be the nicest person in the long run.

GOAL: It's not every time someone hurts you that it's because they are mean, so try to build a tougher shell and be impervious to hurtful attitude.

Day One-Hundred-and-Eighteen: April 28

We are what we repeatedly do; excellence, then, is not an act, but a habit.

–Aristotle

Whatever it is you are doing requires patience and persistence if it's going to become great. You have to keep working at getting better and making sure you never stop. An act is built into a habit only when it is done consistently. For example, taking coffee doesn't become something of a habit in just a day. You must have done it over a while before your body starts demanding for it before everyday activity. Healthy and successful habit can also be developed in the same way and help you build your path to excellence.

GOAL: If you focus and deliver excellence right now, that gives you the best shot at the wonderful future you've got coming. Start doing something you wished continuously and become excellent at it.

Day One-Hundred-and-Nineteen: April 29

Do not mind anything that anyone tells you about anyone else. Judge everyone and everything for yourself.

–Henry James

The 'rumor mill' is one source of information that you should never let shape your opinion. Whether it's about others or a situation. Over the years, I have come in contact with many different scenarios where things are not what they seem at first glance. But with people jumping to a conclusion, it's easy to get mixed up in the crowd. However, you can avoid this by learning to patiently evaluate situations and people and come up with your idea. Even if it's wrong at least, it's your own opinion.

GOAL: When it comes to evaluating others, do it yourself and don't be influenced by what others say.

Day One-Hundred-and-Twenty: April 30

If it's not worth your time, it's not worth your heart.

Anything that you know is a waste of time should not be in your thoughts. Your mind should be a sacred place where the thoughts that would shape your life dwell. Don't let it become a place for malice, hate, fear, or anger to stay.

GOAL: Stay positive with your thoughts, and think things that can transform your life for the better.

MAY

Day One-Hundred-and-Twenty-One: May 1

Ride on someone else's lane and feel the bumps

It can be effortless to judge people from where you stand, but when you put yourself in their shoes, you might not have so many comments about them. In life, it's easy to detach ourselves from reality and become insensitive to what others are feeling. But it's best to consider others and treat them with compassion.

GOAL: Reach out to someone today and offer solace for any tough situation they are going through. What about sending some flowers?

Day One-Hundred-and-Twenty-Two: May 2

Wherever you go, go with all your heart.

– *Confucius*

If we had more people in the world who allow their heart to guide them when making decisions, then the world would be a better place. Staying true to one's heart is one of the ways to achieve one's dreams because it comes from a place of purity and passion without any ulterior motive.

GOAL: Your heart is your most reliable ally, always listen to it when it comes to making decisions.

Day One-Hundred-and-Twenty-Three: May 3

Change is inevitable, and growth is optional.

– John C. Maxwell

There are things in this world that would keep happening, and one of those things is change. It is something that happens to everyone at one stage of life or another. And since there's no stopping it, you can as well use it to your advantage. Changes are an opportunity to grow, but that wouldn't happen if you don't work for it.

GOAL: Is there any phase of your life where you are experiencing change? Try to take it as an opportunity to grow. Think out of the box.

Day One-Hundred-and-Twenty-Four: May 4

You are braver than you believe and stronger than you seem, and smarter than you think.

– *A.A. Milne (Winnie the Pooh)*

Bravery, strength, and intelligence are all features that everyone possesses. The only problem is that a lot of people don't believe this. For example, a rat would never be able to challenge you and get away with it, but you can live in fear of rats and run away whenever you see one. It doesn't still change the fact that in the hierarchy of species, a human is superior to rat. That is precisely the way the world is. If you decide to cower when the situation gets dicey or shy away when the problems seem too complicated, you would never be all you are meant to be. But if you decide to stand up for the things you believe and never back down; only then would you discover how brave, smart, and intelligent you truly are.

GOAL: Never let challenges send you scurrying away, instead of standing up and face them knowing they can never get the better of you. Remember that once you accept the challenges, you can feel the exhilaration of victory.

Day One-Hundred-and-Twenty-Five: May 5

Life is like a mural, and you determine the outcome by choosing your brush, colors, and strokes.

You can decide what you want your life to be like in the next five, ten, and in years to come. You have to be deliberate about things. My life started to take a good shape the day I determined I would never settle for less than the best, and you can do exactly that too. Remember, you are the artist; you control what the mural produce.

GOAL: Write dreams and ambitions for years ahead and start doing something about it. Don't just write and plan, take actions.

Day One-Hundred-and-Twenty-Six: May 6

The question isn't who is going to let me; it's who is going to stop me.

– Ayn Rand

As I started to lose the old me who was saddled with issues and a sucker at many things, I started to attract the attention of 'nay-sayer.' It can be really scary when you have so many people telling you to 'take it slow,' 'don't think too much' or 'you might get stuck.' But the key is to make sure they never get into your head. You can do whatever it is you set out to do, and even if you fail, at least you tried. And remember, failure is just another way of not doing something.

GOAL: Whatever it is you choose to do, don't let anyone tell you, 'you can't.' Get up and do it. The world's admired achievers have been those who have always stayed focused on their goals and have been consistent in their efforts.

Day One-Hundred-and-Twenty-Seven: May 7

Communication skills are only half the battle in leadership and life. If we're honest, the real struggle happens inside our hearts and souls.

– *Nancy Duarte*

My mind was always a field of negative thoughts a while back. I would always have thoughts that make me feel sad through the day and a growing weight that never seemed to leave. But with growth came better inspiration to live differently. And the victories in my life started from the place of my mind. I had to first shift my focus from negative to positive, and this reflected in my overall attitude to life. Your thoughts are vital to what you want to become, win the battle of your mind and watch as you transform.

GOAL: Read book, materials, and do things that only give you positive things to think about.

Day One-Hundred-and-Twenty-Eight: May 8

Now, think of the happiest things. It's the same as having wings.

– Peter Pan

Happy memories bring you a feeling of exhilaration that cannot be compared to anything. You should stay in these thoughts more often; they can give you the power to stay happy no matter what happens. Ride on the wings of happiness, and you would fly above the dark waters of sadness, no matter how deep they are.

GOAL: Think of the happiest experiences you have had. Also think of what you would love to do the most and imagine doing it. Let the thoughts fill your mind through the day and stay in that happy place.

Day One-Hundred-and-Twenty-Nine: May 9

The best part about being alone is that you don't have to answer to anybody. You do what you want.

– Justin Timberlake

Being alone isn't so easy, but it gets better the longer you stay that way. I have come to realize that there are perks to staying alone, and one of them is being able to make decisions that are good for you. You don't have to worry about hurting another person's feeling. And you get to understand yourself even better, become stronger, and find joy and peace at the moment.

GOAL: Find solace in staying with your thoughts. Love yourself!

Day One-Hundred-and-Thirty: May 10

You have within you the patience, and the passion for reaching for the stars and changing the world.

– Harriet Tubman

I was sitting at a coffee shop recently, and I watched as a homeless man pushed his cart around the garbage can picking something I couldn't quite see. It touched something in me, and I ordered another cup of coffee with some bagel to take to him. The smile on his face was priceless, and that was just enough to make my day. No matter the small act of kindness, there is no effort too small to make the world around us a better place. We just have to reach inside of us, get in touch with our human side, and you would be surprised at what you can do.

GOAL: Let empathy be your priority; never leave a situation you could change without trying to make a difference.

Day One-Hundred-and-Thirty-One: May 11

I have realized that the past and future are real illusions, that they exist in the present, which is what there is and all there is.

– *Alan Watts*

Sometimes when I sit down to meditate, I can't quite remember some of the things that happened in the past. This made me come up with the fact that the past doesn't offset the present. We are who we are by what we choose to do in the present.

GOAL: Enjoy every single moment you find yourself in. Leave your phone, shut your computer, and live in the moment.

Day One-Hundred-and-Thirty-Two: May 12

Find joy in the process, not the destination.

It's so easy to look at the far destination and feel burdened, but why not find joy in the journey instead. I have learned that looking back and remembering everything I have ever done to get to where I want gives me joy. So I don't dwell on all the tasks left to do; rather, I find my joy in remembering the thing I have done and using that energy to perform the next task. Remember that it's all a matter of slow and steady.

GOAL: Look at all the achievements you have and celebrate them today. And for the ones still unaccomplished, find joy in what you are doing to get there.

Day One-Hundred-and-Thirty-Three: May 13

Persons of high self-esteem are not driven to make themselves superior to others; they do not seek to prove their value by measuring themselves against a comparative standard. Their joy is being who they are, not in being better than somebody else.

– *Nathaniel Branden*

There are no standards that say you have to be better than everybody. Nobody is saying you have to be perfect. Just enjoy yourself while you do what you love.

GOAL: Enjoy life as you wake up each day. Count your blessings today.

Day One-Hundred-and-Thirty-Four: May 14

If you cannot do great things, do small things in a great way.

– *Napoleon Hill*

It isn't until you become the president of your country that you can start doing great things. Great things don't matter simply because they are great things; they matter because they have an impact on people. However small your circle is, you can do something great today. Just be ready to give your best, and the rest would fall into place.

GOAL: Put your best into whatever you do, no matter how small it is, you will be proud of yourself.

Day One-Hundred-and-Thirty-Five: May 15

Honesty is the first chapter in the book of wisdom.

– Thomas Jefferson

Being honest is not always easy, and people have been in several situations where it would have just been easy to tell a fib and make things simple. But the truth is, a fib doesn't just go away. It invites other lies and can quickly become something of a habit. You have to learn to deal with matters truthfully, though it might not seem like it, it's the best thing to do.

GOAL: Whatever happens, always tell the truth, let your integrity be one of your highest standards.

Day One-Hundred-and-Thirty-Six: May 16

We must let go of the life we planned, so as to accept the one that is waiting for us.

– Joseph Carmpbell

Thinking big, having long and short term goals, and planning for the future are all great things and you should do them. But also try to be flexible, things might not go exactly the way you planned it, but the flexibility allows you to adjust to change and move on.

GOAL: Learn to accept that not everything would work the way you planned it. Be flexible to life. Try different plans ahead.

Day One-Hundred-and-Thirty-Seven: May 17

Worrying is stupid, it's like walking about with an umbrella waiting for it to rain.

– Wiz Khalifa

It's the natural human instinct to feel like something would go wrong, especially when they have had a streak of things going right. There is just always that banging feeling that won't seem to go away that makes us worry. But you can change that. Things don't have to be perfect, and something may truly go wrong, but we can correct our mistakes. That is the beauty of life, and it's that as long as you are alive, you can correct things that go wrong. So it's time to stop worrying and start enjoying everything even if they don't go as smoothly as you have planned.

GOAL: When you start worrying, picture yourself carrying an umbrella and walking under clear skies. Funny, right? Let that thought cheer you up.

Day One-Hundred-and-Thirty-Eight: May 18

Now is the best time to start.

There is no better time than the present. If you have been planning to start something, be it a band, coffee shop, bake sale, or learning to play the piano, stop procrastinating and start now.

GOAL: If you have been planning on starting a business, skill learning, or project, begin immediately.

Day One-Hundred-and-Thirty-Nine: May 19

Endurance is one of the most difficult disciplines, but it is to the one who endures that the final victory comes.

– *Buddha*

Pain and hurt aren't two good things that anyone desires. I had my fair share of each when things got really bad. It was always like they were the only things that rick bottom brought along with it. However, I learned endurance through them. It's not so much as the things that happen to us that shape us; it's how we can endure them and transform the pain into a life-changing experience. You would then have had victory over the hurt.

GOAL: If you are you going through a bad or hurtful situation, think of a way you can turn it into a life-changing experience. It may be just what you need to make your life shine.

Day One-Hundred-and-Forty: May 20

In life you are either a passenger or a pilot, it's your choice.

– Unknown

In life, there is no sitting on the fence. You can either choose to direct your path or let life give you directions. When I started, there was no plan, no resolve, and no clue, it was all just a roller coaster with me going in all directions with 'next to nothing' productivity. But when I decided to grab hold of the steering wheel, things turned out differently. Never let life toss you around, man up and be the boss of your life.

GOAL: Start making decisions that would put you where you want, not where life decides to put you.

Day One-Hundred-and-Forty-One: May 21

Don't be afraid of your fears. They are not there to scare you. They are there to let you know that something is worth it.

– C. Joybell C.

Your fears are not signs for you to stop pushing, instead they are boards that point you into the right direction. Don't stop dreaming or moving toward your goal when you face scary obstacles, instead surmount your fears and keep moving on.

GOAL: Think of all the things you fear about your dreams and draw a road map to surmount them as you go on.

Day One-Hundred-and-Forty-Two: May 22

Dreams are illustrations. from the book your soul is writing about you.

– Marsha Norman

Dreams are great, and they are the motivation that keeps you focused on where you want to be. But they just won't magically happen without you putting an effort. The universe would only help those who are bold enough to step out and do something about their dreams.

GOAL: We all have a purpose for living, but we would never realize them if we do nothing.

Day One-Hundred-and-Forty-Three: May 23

The more grateful I am, the more beauty I see.

– Mary Davis

Gratitude is the key to true happiness. When I look back at my life, I am grateful for the things that I have and for every single person that is around me. My friends, my colleagues, my family, and every single person that had to lend me a hand when I needed help. My journey hasn't been smooth, but I have had people who helped me get out of every kink on the road.

GOAL: Think about every point in your life where someone has helped out and thank them.

Day One-Hundred-and-Forty-Four: May 24

Everyone has a crown. It's there, but it's invisible.

We have to learn to celebrate our victories no matter how little they are. No matter what other people think about you, always remember that you came this far. Each plan, each activity is getting you closer to excellence, but never be too concerned with the destination that you forget to celebrate the journey.

GOAL: Recognize your hard work and celebrate your creativity.

Day One-Hundred-and-Forty-Five: May 25

Like the moon, come out from behind the clouds! Shine.

– Buddha

It is up to you to shine your light or cower behind darkness. You can control your thoughts and actions so that you are a light to the world around you, an inspiration in hardship and an illumination when all hope seems lost.

GOAL: Your simplest actions could inspire others, so never carry any sore emotions around. Be who you truly are and shine your brightest light!

Day One-Hundred-and-Forty-Six: May 26

Time will heal the pain. Maybe not today and maybe not tomorrow; but one day it will all go away. Stay strong!

– Katie Dickinson

Writing from the point of a reader can introduce some sort of anonymity that makes it seem that the writer is so invincible and powerful. But trust me when I say there are days I have cried, felt pain, and been completely hopeless. But what makes me a better person is that I get up each time to face life with renewed strength and make sure to fight to win. Eventually, the pain goes away, just like the sun comes out after the storm, no matter how long it takes.

GOAL: No matter the hurt or pain you are going through, find solace in the fact that it will pass. Watch a comedy movie, make a popcorn, and enjoy yourself.

Day One-Hundred-and-Forty-Seven: May 27

The only limits that exist are the ones you set.

Someone once said, your passion can take you anywhere. Well, I agree. When you let the passion within you find expression, there is no limit to what you can do. And you can choose to fuel it as far as it would go.

GOAL: Never limit your dreams, dream big and dream wide. Only big dreams have the power to move our soul.

Day One-Hundred-and-Forty-Eight: May 28

Do your part, and the rest would fall into place.

– Anonymous

Volunteering is one of the best ways to make the world around you a better place. It's the little token you can give to the community to help. I've had the privilege of serving in charities, advocating for bullying, and attending charities for orphanages.

GOAL: Volunteer at any opportunity you have; it's a way of giving back to the world around you. Spread love and compassion.

Day One-Hundred-and-Forty-Nine: May 29

You are twice armed if you fight with faith.

– Plato

Believing in yourself is the best motivation that can get you to where you dream of being. Whatever you do, never get to the point where you lose your faith. There would be struggles, challenges, and plenty of criticism, but it's your faith that gets you past them.

GOAL: Believe so much in what you do that nothing holds you back. You are braver than you think and more talented than you know!

Day One-Hundred-and-Fifty: May 30

When you are content to be simply yourself and don't compare or compete, everyone will respect you.

–*Lao Tzu*

There are moments when we feel lost to ourselves and look for meaning in other people's lives. Our colleagues, our roommates, or even strangers become the standard that defines how happy or sad we are. I can only tell you that you would live a miserable life if this is how your life is. Being inspired by someone because of their good taste and value is acceptable, but it becomes something else if you don't feel fulfilled when you measure up to them. Becoming someone else won't bring you joy, you have to discover that in being yourself.

GOAL: Be humble and find happiness in being who you are. Be nice with yourself.

Day One-Hundred-and-Fifty-One: May 31

Your intentions for doing good are as crucial as the act itself.

When it comes to doing good, you can do it for the wrong intentions. The purpose is important when you are volunteering, donating to the orphanage, or helping a friend out. You shouldn't do these things because you want recognition or need something in return. Give without expecting and receive without forgetting. I discovered that some of the best fulfilment I have found when doing good is doing it anonymously and from our heart.

GOAL: Donate, send a caring message, or perform an act of kindliness today.

JUNE

Day One-Hundred-and-Fifty-Two: June 1

A friend is someone who gives you total freedom to be yourself.

– Jim Morrison

If you ever look around you and you find only people who look down on you and make you feel inadequate, then it's time for a change. True friends are those that bring the best out of you while making you feel good through the process. They are there for you when you laugh and console you when you cry.

GOAL: Stay away from people that make you feel down. Surround yourself with people that inspire and encourage you.

Day One-Hundred-and-Fifty-Three: June 2

You miss 100 percent of the shots you never take.

– Wayne Gretzky

Most things we never do are dreams ghosts waiting to haunt us. When we look at the past and remember those opportunities we missed, we are sometimes filled with regrets. One of the keys to happiness is never to let opportunities pass you by without taking a shot at it. You should not be too scared, worried, or afraid to try; the only fear you should have is having an opportunity and letting it pass you by.

GOAL: Don't let a day go by without making the best use of it. The best memories we have are those where we lived our dreams.

Day One-Hundred-and-Fifty-Four: June 3

Never let go of the child inside of you, it's the creative beauty the universe cherishes.

It's always amazing how the best form of creativity is that that comes from the innermost part of our being. But we carried away a lot, and we get in the habit of doing so much damage to this creative part that it becomes buried under all the load if our heartaches. Think of it like telling a 3-year-old to carry two donkeys, it's unthinkable right. Well, that is what you are doing to your inner self. The world loves beauty and recognizes one when they see it, so take care of yourself because the world needs it.

GOAL: Take care of yourself and never let life's many worries to get the best of you.

Day One-Hundred-and-Fifty-Five: June 4

Two things define you. Your patience when you have nothing and your attitude when you have everything.

– Anonymous

There are two crucial times in our lives, and that is when we have nothing and when we have everything. It's so easy to have some preferences and moral standards when there is no money to indulge in excesses. Then we can point fingers and speak freely of the excesses some people indulge in. But when the storms pass, and there is enough money, then we find out we are not so better ourselves. What defines us should be our circumstances; it should be a strong definition of your values and attitude that absolutely nothing can change.

GOAL: Think of all the times you have behaved differently in different situations.

Day One-Hundred-and-Fifty-Six: June 5

Talent is given, greatness is earned.

I have talents, and they have been there for as long as I can remember. I can play soccer seamlessly, I could do so many things at the same time and do some other thing smoothly. But I'm not Pele, neither am I William Shakespeare, this is because greatness is not achieved by merely having a talent. Greatness is a function of hard work mixed with passion.

GOAL: If you want to achieve greatness, be determined to work hard.

Day One-Hundred-and-Fifty-Seven: June 6

The wisest mind has something yet to learn.

– George Santana

No matter how good you are, you still have a lot of things to learn. I have been taught some of the most crucial lessons in my life by those that are my mentees. It doesn't matter who, never look down on anyone.

GOAL: Go out every day with a mind open to learning.

Day One-Hundred-And-Fifty-Eight: June 7

How I feel about myself is more important than how I look. Feeling confident, being comfortable in your skin—that's what makes you beautiful.

– Bobbi Brown

When it comes to how you look, your opinion is the most important. As longs as you feel confident and beautiful in your skin, you would live a happy life. We have seen people who have one or two disabilities still living the best of their lives, and this gives me the inspiration to do likewise. If they can face each day with bright faces and high esteem then what's stopping us?

GOAL: "We look back to be grateful"—appreciate what you have, think of those who have less and are still grateful.

Day One-Hundred-and-Fifty-Nine: June 8

The more you love, the more you become lovable.

– *Osho*

Love is one of the most significant act any human can display. It not only leaves you at peace, but it also gives you a connection to those around you. We are united as humans, not only because we are the same, but because of each of our differences. So no matter how unrelated you are to people around you, love yourself, love them, and enjoy the great circle of love you give to life.

GOAL: Focus on loving everyone around you, including yourself.

Day One-Hundred-and-Sixty: June 9

We are one of the luckiest people to live because we have guides and journals that show us the way to go.

This generation is one of the best you can live in. There is so much to guide and lead you to success. No matter the area of specialty you choose to delve into, there is a book, a course, and even mentors to take you on the journey. It's essential to learn from all of these available materials. And don't forget to show respect and gratitude for the availability of all these resources.

GOAL: Be an explorer today. Don't take anything you touch, hear or see for granted. Be willing to look closely at everything and become a student of your environment. Check for books at the store that contain relevant information.

Day One-Hundred-and-Sixty-One: June 10

Some people look for a beautiful place. Others make a place beautiful.

–Hazrat Inayat Khan

Too often, we wait for other people to do something to make the world around us better. When you get to a place, don't wait for someone to do something you can do. Be the sunshine everywhere you are.

GOAL: Decide today to add that dose of life everywhere you go. Show how amazing you are!

Day One-Hundred-and-Sixty-Two: June 11

I can't change the direction of the wind, but I can adjust my sails always to reach my destination.

– Jimmy Dean

We can't control everything in life, but we can make the best out of each opportunity. I have learnt that what matters is not all the opportunities, but what we do while we wait for that one perfect opportunity. That is all you need to ride your way to success.

GOAL: Stop waiting for things to change, work on yourself while waiting, and then when the right time comes, don't be found snoozing.

Day One-Hundred-and-Sixty-Three: June 12

A successful man is one who can lay a firm foundation with the bricks others have thrown at him.

–David Brinkley

One of the best feelings you would ever get is showing critics that you are getting better in spite of all the disbelief they throw at you. The first time I experienced this exhilaration, I told myself I would never let anyone control my progress, no matter who they are. It's just better to spend time showing YOURSELF and them how far you really can go.

GOAL: If anyone have ever told you, you can't, prove them wrong today. Yes, you can!

Day One-Hundred-and-Sixty-Four: June 13

Be thankful for what you have; you'll end up having more. If you concentrate on what you don't have, you will never, ever have enough.

– Oprah Winfrey

We all have more than we can ever think, but we lose track of happiness because we focus on the things we don't have. All it just takes to be happy sometimes is to make a conscious effort and write down all that you possess, and your thoughts would start changing from positive to negative.

GOAL: Make a list of the negative thoughts making you sad, then for each thought write something positive. Now, stand in from of the mirror and read the positive ones to yourself.

Day One-Hundred-and-Sixty-Five: June 14

Reaching out for help is not a sign of weakness, it's just a sign that you are only human.

Sometimes we feel burdened by the weight of our experiences, but we get so ashamed of sharing them that we let them eat at us slowly. But you shouldn't let it. I battle with depression for some time while I was going through hard times. I kept it all to myself because I didn't want to feel embarrassed about sharing my personal issues with someone else. But in the end, getting help assisted my burdens a lot. And I'm grateful I did, or who knows I might not be writing this.

GOAL: When it gets really tough, seek help fast. Surely someone is going to support you.

Day One-Hundred-and-Sixty-Six: June 15

Be patient; good things take time.

– Anonymous

It can be so hard to be patient, especially if you have already had to wait for so long. But you have to trust that patience produces the best fruit. It's sometimes necessary to wait for years just to achieve what you want, but it just means the reward would be better than what you anticipated.

GOAL: Patiently trust the process while you wait for your dreams and aspirations to be fulfilled.

Day One-Hundred-and-Sixty-Seven: June 16

You can either stand for something or fall for everything.

Emulating the values of great people is good, but it's the opposite of good if we feel the need to follow every single person we meet. You can't stand for every single thing in the world. Mostly, it's better to pick your side and stick to it. It would save you from living a stressful and confusing life. And it's not so much about admiring those values, and it's acting them out that really counts.

GOAL: Think of 5 people you think are great, write out their values and choose to emulate them.

Day One-Hundred-and-Sixty-Eight: June 17

It is our choices that show what we truly are, far more than our abilities.

– J. K. Rowling

One of the lessons life has taught is that people are not who they are by what they choose but by what they can do. Sometimes, it is possible to be restricted by certain conditions, such as finances, when making choices. There could also be a limited amount of varieties to choose from. But abilities don't depend on what you have around, and it is simply an innate feature that shows who you really are.

GOAL: Try not to judge people based on what they wear, what they choose to listen to, or the kind of movies they like, instead of judge them based on their attitudes.

Day One-Hundred-and-Sixty-Nine: June 18

Many of life's failures are people who did not realize how close they were to success when they gave up.

– Thomas A. Edison

When it comes to not giving up, you can trust Thomas Edison when he gives you a pointer or two. The man failed so many times but refused to let it stop his dream. What this taught me is that every experience or situation happens to help us grow and learn humility. We should not be discouraged by our failure, because though they might change you, they should not bring you down. Whenever anyone talks down on you because you failed at something, then it's not you, it's just a projection about the insecurities they have about themselves.

GOAL: Do not let life's challenges weigh you down if you have failed at anything, be determined to get back up and try again.

Day One-Hundred-and-Seventy: June 19

Life is the first gift, love is the second, and understanding the third.

– Marge Piercy

The best gift life can hand you is living, because as long as you are alive, you can give love as much as you want. And love comes with understanding; you cannot find someone and not understand them. So the three gifts are there to help you live every day happy you are here, love everyone, and accommodate their imperfections.

GOAL: Life is not about perfection; it is learning to be grateful while you live and extending love to others.

Day One-Hundred-and-Seventy-One: June 20

Life would be tragic if it weren't funny.

– Stephen Hawking

It's absolutely true that we have to enjoy what little time we have here on earth, else it would all be for nothing. The best memories that shape some of our best smiles are those we had while having fun with people. So try not to get so hung up on so many meetings or burdened by small stuff. Enjoy life while you can, and have fun living in the present.

GOAL: Take time off to spend time together with the ones you love. Go for a movie, book a roller coaster ride, and make fun memories.

Day One-Hundred-And-Seventy-Two: June 21

The best way to live is to live true to your own self.

There is a pressure that comes with living that can make us lose ourselves in the process. The stress we go through each day can remove the accountability we owe ourselves, but one thing that I always remember is how I owe myself the truth. Am I living my best life? Or am I just allowing myself to be bossed around by life's many troubles? These questions keep me in check and help me stay true to who I am.

GOAL: Never lose yourself in the battles life throws at you, instead pick yourself up each time without leaving any part of who you are.

Day One-Hundred-And-Seventy-Three: June 22

Keep your face to the sunshine, and you cannot see a shadow.

– Helen Keller

I saw this quote, and it instantly did something to me. Helen Keller couldn't see, but she hadn't lost the power to be a visionary. She was able to find that light that exists inside every human, and she shined it on the perspective of everyone who cares to read about her or listen. It's an attitude that motivates me, and it should motivate you too.

GOAL: Don't let what is happening on the outside to trouble you; focus on your inner self and find that light within you. Shine brightly!

Day One-Hundred-and-Seventy-Four: June 23

Little by little, day by day, what is meant for you will find its way.

Whatever it is we are working toward, we can achieve it when we take little steps each day. When I spend so much time working toward achieving a goal, I lose myself in time. This is because I love what I do, but that doesn't mean I won't take breaks or days off. You can't achieve all in one day.

GOAL: It's better to take breaks while you work on projects or at your job. It helps to refresh the mind and keep you healthy.

Day One-Hundred-and-Seventy-Five: June 24

The first half of life is devoted to forming a healthy ego, the second half is going inward and letting go of it.

– *Carl Jung*

Our egos are not what shape us to be who we are. We have to take responsibility for our actions. When we want to make decisions, we have to learn to put aside our ambitions and think about what is best for everyone, even though it might not feed our ego.

GOAL: Take responsibility for every decision you make and remember that it's not always just about you. Be compassionate to others.

Day One-Hundred-and-Seventy-Six: June 25

Make no promise you cannot keep because unfulfilled promises are an injury to the soul.

There are times in the past when I made promises to people but forgot to fulfil them. But one incident that changed it was when it almost cost the friendship I hold dear. We do not sometimes realize that we build people hope when we make promises and then dash it when we fail to fulfil. So, when you make promises, try to fulfil them as soon as possible.

GOAL: If you have made any promise you have not fulfilled, try to fulfil it immediately, and if it's not possible, then write it where you can see it every day until you do it.

Day One-Hundred-and-Seventy-Seven: June 26

Pride brings nothing but pain.

Being proud does not help anyone; in the long run, you are going to need help. But your pride would not let you ask. Pride also breaks relationships and hinders the ability to learn. There is no advantage to pride, none at all.

GOAL: When you need something, ask people around. Don't let haughtiness rob you off from gaining from people around you.

Day One-Hundred-and-Seventy-Eight: June 27

Limit your 'always' and your 'nevers.'

– Amy Poehler

Living a balanced life has been one of the best ways I have learned to live. There is no hurry to make promises you cannot fulfil, and you aren't trying to please everyone by doing what you do. Realizing that you control your own life is a great realization, and you would live much more peacefully that way.

GOAL: Don't make promises just because you want to please people. Do what brings your peace above all.

Day One-Hundred-and-Seventy-Nine: June 28

When I dare to be powerful—to use my strength in the service of my vision, then it becomes less and less important whether I am afraid.

– Audre Lorde

Fear is a thing of the mind, and it would get you far away from your dream as possible. But you can overcome it. Some years ago, I used to have a fear of failing before I even started something up, but I learned that the more I think about doing it, the more I desire to do. The mind is very amazing, because the more you do this, the more it removes the negatives and motivates you to go for it. Fuel your passion, and your fear would be insignificant.

GOAL: Write down everything fear is stopping you from achieving, read it out every day, and start thinking of how it would be when you are done. You will find a solution and brighter plans ahead.

Day One-Hundred-and-Eighty: June 29

Integrity is the most valuable and respected quality of leadership. Always keep your word.

– Brian Tracy

Don't say things just for the fun of saying them, you have to make sure you think before speaking. You can't be a leader if you say things that are not meant all the time.

GOAL: Learn to be cautious when talking. Mean what you say, say what you mean.

Day One-Hundred-and-Eighty-One: June 30

How time flies…

Time waits for no one. It's half of the year already and the first day looks just like yesterday. When we get to this part of the year, I have learned to check my books and reevaluate my goals, dreams, and aspirations. It's never too late to start everything you set out for, but it would be tomorrow.

GOAL: Go back to your to-do list and diaries, look at the things you have to achieve and work on those you are yet to.

JULY

Day One-Hundred-And-Eighty-Two: July 1

Above all, be the heroine of your life, not the victim.

– Nora Ephron

Life has a way of happening to us all, and it can be at inopportune moments too. But the way you handle it when it does solely depend on you. Never let other people decide your fate, don't leave everything in the hands of someone else. Get up, do something about that situation, and watch as you become the hero of your own story like I did.

GOAL: Take charge of anything that has to do with you and never back down till you win.

Day One-Hundred-and-Eighty-Three: July 2

Keep on going, and the chances are that you will stumble on something, perhaps when you are least expecting it. I never heard of anyone ever stumbling on something sitting down.

– Charles F. Kettering

Over time I have heard so many things about finding purpose and living a fulfilled life. Well, at first I got confused because I love doing so many things, I couldn't decide which was my purpose. But then I was at a restaurant, and someone had scribbled 'keep pushing forward' on the door. That's when it dawned on me that finding purpose is not necessarily having a big dream where everything suddenly becomes clear. Purpose can be found in doing something with persistence and perseverance, and clarity will be better as you go.

GOAL: If you don't have a clarity of purpose. Look for something you at least like doing and persist at it.

Day One-Hundred-and-Eighty-Four: July 3

You don't choose your family. They are God's gift to you, as you are to them.

– Desmond Tutu

Friends, colleagues, and well-wishers are all vital to me. But I can't forget the ones that have always been in the picture. Right from when the world couldn't see me until the present moment. My family have always been those with me through my worst moments and my best times. They have always been a shoulder of comfort and a heart to share my laughter with. Those are the people to celebrate every time you get a chance. Never go so far away from them because they are always there no matter how far you go.

GOAL: Take time to visit your family and celebrate them whenever you get the chance.

Day One-Hundred-and-Eighty-Five: July 4

Never despise the days of your youth.

As we grow older, our body starts to lose the exuberance it used to possess, little by little. No matter the exercise or regimen we adopt, there would be a difference in how much you can do while we were young, and when we get old. So live life now, go to a rave, take a hike, run, and enjoy every bit of it. 'Cause it's the memories that would fuel your old years and entertain your mind.

GOAL: Whatever you can do now, do it before it's too late. You don't want to live in regrets over unlived dreams.

Day One-Hundred-and-Eighty-Six: July 5

"Hakuna Matata." It means no worries!

– The Lion King

Living without worries does not mean living a carefree life; it simply means not allowing the troubles of yesterday to ruin the progress you should make today. Never give your past power over your future. Let what you do now decide that.

GOAL: Don't let the problems you faced hinder you from achieving greatness. Whatever you have been through, it's time to get over it and move on.

Day One-Hundred-and-Eighty-Seven: July 6

You've got a friend in me.

– Toy Story

A lot of people have been there for me in my times of need. And it's only natural that my shoulder is there for them to rest on in their times of trouble. Always be there for those that had been there for you at one time or the other. Not because you owe them but because kindness is part of our nature.

GOAL: Reach out to someone that has been there for you and comfort them if they are going through hardships.

Day One-Hundred-and-Eighty-Eight: July 7

However, many holy words you read, however many you speak, what good will they do you if you do not act on upon them?

– *Buddha*

When I was young, we were always asked in school to do a presentation of what we would like to be when we grow up. And a lot of people would take the doctor's uniform, others would take the engineer's hat, and some would wear the lawyer's suit. But all of that was theatrics, and a lot of us aren't those things now. That taught me something. We wouldn't get to where we want by wishing or speaking or reading motivational quotes. It is our actions that really make us who we want to be.

GOAL: Act on your words today, and for every quote you read that applies to you, don't let the day go by without acting it out. Make your dreams come true!

Day One-Hundred-and-Eighty-Nine: July 8

Sometimes you have to take two steps back to take ten steps forward.

– Nipsey Hussle

Yes, you shouldn't let your past decide who you become, and it shouldn't hold you down either. But you can learn from it. To go forward, sometimes, you look at the experience of the past and take one or two lessons from it. Every failure is a lesson learned, and every success can still be improved on.

GOAL: Think of your past and write down the lessons you have learned from it, but never let it weigh you down or make you sad. Remember that you have become a greater person.

Day One-Hundred-and-Ninety: July 9

When you throw dirt, you lose ground.

– Texan Proverb

It can be very difficult to make the right choices sometimes, especially when in tempting situations. The best way to treat people who have been unfair to you seems to be the same way they treat you. But wouldn't that just breed a whole circle of pain, so it's better to break the circle than fuel it.

GOAL: Don't respond to unfairness with the same attitude; instead, calmly tell the person how would they feel if you treated them the same way.

Day One-Hundred-and-Ninety-One: July 10

There is no mistake in the universe, everything exists for a reason.

Each time I face a challenge that seems discouraging, the thought that everything is for a reason keeps me going. There are over 6 billion people in the universe, and if I'm going through a circumstance, then it's happening to me and not the billions of people remaining in the universe. So instead of shying away, I take the challenge head-on and face it with that perspective.

GOAL: Inspire yourself to overcome any challenge you are going through. Surely it's going to inspire others as well.

Day One-Hundred-and-Ninety-Two: July 11

I must be a mermaid, Rango. I have no fear of depths and a great fear of shallow living.

– *Anais Nin*

Our capabilities are sometimes scary, especially when we see how far we can go with the potentials we possess. But with great power comes even greater responsibility. Your responsibility is to control how far you plunge; you can't control the waves and torrent, but you can have one hand on the floater.

GOAL: Be responsible for what you do with your resources.

Day One-Hundred-and-Ninety-Three: July 12

It's the little things in life.

Ever seen how our little ones smile at the littlest of funny expression, that is because they find humor in the simplest of gesture. Growing up chips away our sense of humor little by little until we have to attend a stand-up comedy to have a good laugh. But that shouldn't be, learn to find happiness in the little things in life. That way you can live life happy and cherish each moment.

GOAL: Try to loosen up, being uptight wouldn't get you anywhere. Laughing is always the best form of therapy.

Day One-Hundred-and-Ninety-Four: July 13

Low self-esteem is like driving through life with your hand-break on.

– Maxwell Maltz

Being bullied is a terrible thing, especially for a young person who is just learning the principle of the world around her/him. It builds up a view of a selfish and wicked world, and causes them to limit their expression and become less of themselves. There have even been cases of depression because of the low self-esteem that bullying breeds. And the cyber world has now given the bullies the privilege of being anonymous while they intrude and pillage someone else's esteem. It's up to us to build our self-esteem and then to stand up for others who are struggling.

GOAL: Help out with counselling and standing up for youth who have been bullied or have low self-esteem due to the experience.

Day One-Hundred-and-Ninety-Five: July 14

I don't need a friend who changes when I change and who nods when I nod; my shadow does that much better.

– Plutarch

Your friends are supposed to be people that motivate you to do more. They should spur you on to greatness. The moment you discover that the people around you are satisfied with all your choices, with no hint of advice or rebuke, then you need to be careful.

GOAL: Choose your friend carefully, they can determine how far you go.

Day One-Hundred-and-Ninety-Six: July 15

Change your perspective, change your life.

Some days do not begin the way I would have loved. They have this vibe that is totally on the wrong level. It's so bad that it even affects some other things during the day. But I have learned a simple trick that works like magic. I simply start the day again. And I don't mean I go back to bed and sleep off the feeling. What I do is to find a peaceful spot, close my eyes, and shift my perspective to the things that give me joy. I remember the blessings life has handed out to me, and the achievement I have. It's like a chain reaction; it gets my mood up and fuels the rest of my day.

GOAL: Start a meditation journal, where you write down your happy thoughts while you meditate. Download meditation apps to guide you through.

Day One-Hundred-and-Ninety-Seven: July 16

The trouble with most of us is that we'd rather be ruined by praise than saved by criticism.

– *Norman Vincent Peale*

In life, not everyone would love to praise your work. But some criticism needs to get your attention. There is a bit of truth in every lie, so you can try to look at some of the things people criticize you about and weigh it. Critics are mostly seen as those who want to tear you down, but when the people you hold dear to your heart throw criticism your way, then maybe it's time to reevaluate your approach to certain things.

GOAL: Creative criticism is a good type of criticism; it helps you work hard at improving your act.

Day One-Hundred-and-Ninety-Eight: July 17

Your ability to see will never broaden when you only see yourself.

– Shannon L. Alder

You should take care of yourself as best as you can but never let it turn into an obsession. The more of only yourself that you see, the less your vision would be. Seeing something from the view of others gives you the ability to make things better. So yes it's all about you, and you are critical, but sometimes leave space for contingency, to include others in your world.

GOAL: Whatever motivation you are following, try to understand that you must find a balance.

Day One-Hundred-and-Ninety-Nine: July 18

Leave your ego at the door every morning, and just do some truly great work. Few things will make you feel better than a job brilliantly done.

– *Robin S. Sharma*

Journeying through life brings us to a lot of stages where we have to get better than we were. But one thing we must be careful of is letting our ego take a ride with us. The damage it does isn't just to us, and it hurts the relationships we are supposed to build and nip at our integrity. Every day, wake up and consciously leave your ego while you go out and work.

GOAL: Take care of your ego daily; never let it gain control of you. Practice gratitude and enjoy silent moments with yourself.

Day Two-Hundred: July 19

Baby steps count, too, as long as you're moving forward.

– *Chris Gardner*

If you are recovering from hurt from the past, then you don't need to feel in a hurry to be over it. Recovery is a process that takes time, and you are not competing against anyone. Go at your own pace, no matter how slow. You might even feel like you are not making progress and want to go back. But never give up, no matter how small you move, don't ever go back. Look forward and keep pushing on.

GOAL: Recovery is a process you need to go through in your own time, never compare your process to someone else. Just be at peace and celebrate each little milestone you accomplish, no matter how small.

Day Two-Hundred-and-One: July 20

Where I am is where I need to be.

When you look back at how everything has worked to bring you here, you realize that you are exactly where you need to be. All my experiences were leading me to this moment, and there's no better place to be than in this moment of happiness.

GOAL: Look back and think about all that you did to get where you are. If you are happy, then you have accomplished more than you think.

Day Two-Hundred-and-Two: July 21

Without pain, without sacrifice, we would have nothing.

– Fight Club

There is a way pain makes us lose all hope of better days. It's always hard to imagine a better life, especially when the hurt is still fresh. But there is always hope, and you have to squint more to see it. The more time you go through the pain, the brighter the light gets until you walk out into a beautiful day. Always face pain with encouragement that someday, it would be a memory painted on some beautiful picture.

GOAL: Don't let pain keep the possibility of recovery away from your mind. Never be void of hope. Remember that the pain makes you stronger than ever before.

Day Two-Hundred-and-Three: July 22

Communication is the key to better relationships.

I have gotten to points in my life where I almost lost those who were important to me. Not because we had a conflict of interest or arguments, but because I got so immersed in what I was working on, I became too busy for them and for everything else. It's not rocket science when people keep walking in and out of our lives. There is just a lack of communication which gets worse over time and eventually keeps you apart forever. Never let that happen to you.

GOAL: Have you been neglecting some people in your life? Take time to reach out to them today. You could take them out for coffee, go visiting, or make a phone call.

Day Two-Hundred-and-Four: July 23

Follow your bliss and the universe will open doors where there were only walls.

– Joseph Campbell

The universe has a way of using vague situations to reach out to us. However, only someone with an open mind would see this. Never be too wound up to see the happiness that lies everywhere you turn.

GOAL: Find fulfilment and happiness in everything you do.

Day Two-Hundred-and-Five: July 24

Sometimes it takes a good fall to really know where to stand.

– Hayley Williams

Falling is not the problem most times. I have learned that falling is a part of life, but what matters is to fall in the best way possible. If I had taken the need to seek help as a sign of weakness, I might have never gotten out of the failure that plagued me for years. The hardest part is not failing; it's getting back up and preparing to fail again.

GOAL: The fear of failure can prevent you from achieving a lot, overcome that fear today.

Day Two-Hundred-and-Six: July 25

Tension is who you think you should be, relaxation is who you are.

– Chinese Proverb

The Chinese proverbs reflect the way to live in your skin without feeling your soul about to jump out. You have objectives, aspirations, and dreams, but you also have a life to live. Don't ruin the present moment by being scared of what the future holds. Live in the now and enjoy it.

GOAL: Plan a vacation, even if it's for a weekend, and relax.

Day Two-Hundred-and-Seven: July 26

There's a time for daring, and there is a time for caution, and a wise man understands which is called for.

– John Keating

I have read loads of books and heard a lots of advices, but it is important to note that not every knowledge should be applied. The key to being successful is to know how to balance things out and use the exact required action for each situation. So never rush into any situation without first evaluating and obtaining the right tool necessary.

GOAL: Always think before you act, don't go headlong into territories you are not familiar with.

Day Two-Hundred-and-Eight: July 27

Compassion is the radicalism of our time.

– Dalai Lama

We all have the ability to forgive others, no matter what they have done to us. It's not a sign of weakness to be so forgiving; rather, it's a sign of strength. What you are saying to the world is that nothing is as important as the peace of the world around you.

GOAL: Determine to be compassionate to those around you.

Day Two-Hundred-and-Nine: July 28

The successful warrior is the average man, with laser-like focus.

– Bruce Lee

No successful man was born that way. They labored for years, working hard and putting their best into what they do. Whatever it is you are doing, put everything you've got into it and never be swayed by the circumstances that would come up. Just focus on your goals, and you would soon be rolling with the big leagues.

GOAL: Try not to lose focus while you work hard at what you love. Always do your best.

Day Two-Hundred-and-Ten: July 29

Don't criticize what you can't understand.

– Bob Dylan

It can be so easy to criticize something from afar. I love pop music and classical music, but that doesn't mean I'm against those who love other types of music. My lack of interest in it is not their fault or because the music is not good, it's because I made a choice, consciously or unconsciously, not to. I should not make that the headache of someone else.

GOAL: Stick to the things that you love and try never to criticize people from afar until you understand them.

Day Two-Hundred-and-Eleven: July 30

Love like there is never going to be another chance to do it.

Everywhere I find myself, I try as much as possible to be calm, reasonable, and lovable. You never know when the last opportunity to love is. So why waste all that love built inside of you. Go out and give love with your words and your action. Trust me; you won't regret it.

GOAL: Always show love with your actions, not just with empty words.

Day One-Hundred-and-Twelve: July 31

No matter what happens, life goes on.

No one wishes to lose a loved one or suffer grief in any way, but tragedy is part of life and it's something we have to deal with. The squeezing of heart, hopelessness, and tears would pass, and there would be brighter days again. Trust me when I say, you would feel better.

GOAL: Grief is a terrible thing, but you would get over it—time heals every scar, no matter how deep.

AUGUST

Day Two-Hundred-and-Thirteen: August 1

To achieve fame with cruelty is simple; to achieve it with kindness is rare.

– Carmine Savastano

There is so much evil in the world today, and most of them are just because of the lust for power. But looking back in time, we never celebrate those that are famous for their cruelty. Instead, we celebrate leaders who used their fame for the good of all humanities. We even name monuments for them and set aside days to celebrate them. This tells us one thing, that cruelty is never celebrated, the things you would be remembered for are the selfless acts you rendered to humanity.

GOAL: On the way up, don't kick people down the ladder, instead build bridges that bring people to the top.

Day Two-Hundred-and-Fourteen: August 2

Don't tell me the sky is the limit when there are footprints on the moon.

The old saying that says "…and the sky would be your limit" is outdated. Now with man conquering the moon, it tells you that the sky shouldn't be the end of it, it should be the beginning. Life can be very good to us and allow us to get to some heights, but never be satisfied being comfortable in the same place for too long. There is more and never stop, even when you get to the peak.

GOAL: Don't be too comfortable because you are in a place of authority. Don't stop until you can genuinely say you have achieved greatness.

Day Two-Hundred-and-Fifteen: August 3

I am not ashamed of my past. I'm actually really proud. I know I made a lot of mistakes, but they, in turn, were my life lessons.

– Drew Barrymore

There are so many instances where I have made mistakes in life, sometimes one mistake leads to another, and you are at the wrong destination before you know it. But I never allow that to define me. I'm proud of what I became even with so many mistakes to talk about. I'm not perfect, but I made my imperfection into a beautiful picture worth admiring.

GOAL: Don't be ashamed of the mistakes you have made before; be proud of what you have become. You might not have made it if not for them.

Day Two-Hundred-and-Sixteen: August 4

Our ship should steer in the direction of our destination, not in the direction other sailors are steering.

At sea, the captain holds a compass and steers his ship in the direction that would lead to the final destination. Well, that is precisely how life is; you must make sure that you are not following the crowd. Live honestly in what you believe, not what in others want you to believe.

GOAL: Your ideas and opinion make you unique, never let go of them.

Day Two-Hundred-and-Seventeen: August 5

In every success story, you will find someone who has made a courageous decision.

– Peter F. Drucker

If anyone ever tells you that you can't achieve your dreams, there is no need to prove them wrong. All you need to do is to believe that you can. When you get to daring situations, make bold decisions. Let your courage guide you as you move forward.

GOAL: You deserve to be happy. Let that be your motivation.

Day Two-Hundred-and-Eighteen: August 6

Selfish—a judgment readily passed by those who have never tested their own power of sacrifice.

– George Eliot

Judging others is quite easy from afar, and sometimes it is because we have not experienced what that person is going through. Try not to pass judgment on people you don't know. There was a time in my life where I was going through some physical pain, and it made me cranky. And if you had met me then, you would think me annoying, but that was not it, it was only the pain.

GOAL: Whatever you are passing through, try not to let it define you. The first impression is not always right!

Day Two-Hundred-and-Nineteen: August 7

I always get to where I'm going by walking away from where I have been.

– Winnie the Pooh

Sometimes we are so comfortable in pain that it becomes our second nature. Then letting it go seems daunting, but if you want to move forward, you have to let go of the past. You won't get anywhere by staying in the same place, the only way to do that is to move forward.

GOAL: Every pain and hurt that you are holding on to, let it go and truly free yourself.

Day Two-Hundred-and-Twenty: August 8

Start from the easiest and move all the way to the top, where the hardest is.

The solution is not always supposed to be hard, and there can be some simple solutions to various challenges. 'There is no easy way out' does always work all the time; sometimes, all you just need to do is hold the door, open it, and walk through to the other side.

GOAL: When you want to solve any problem, try solving it from the simplest method to the hardest route.

Day Two-Hundred-and-Twenty-One: August 9

Humility is not thinking less of yourself, it's thinking of yourself less.

– C. S. Lewis

I once noticed a woman looking at her phone, repeatedly confused and looking dejected on the street. I stopped and asked her what was wrong. Apparently, she was a bit lost, so I offered to take her where she was going. The look of gratitude on her face is one of the loveliest things I have seen till date. We must do the simple things that keep the life around us up and radiant.

GOAL: Lookout for someone who needs help today and help them even if it means going out of your way.

Day Two-Hundred-and-Twenty-Two: August 10

Creativity is inventing, experimenting, growing, taking risks, breaking the rules, making mistakes, and having fun.

– Mary Lou Cook

I remember there was a time when it was difficult for me to try new things. I would think of the cost, the time, and the resources I would have to waste. But then it was because I didn't understand that creativity is experimenting and even if you fail, you still had fun doing something you love.

GOAL: Don't let fear stop you from being creative, just do that thing you love and have fun at it. The key is never to take it too seriously, and in time, you would do something extraordinary.

Day Two-Hundred-and-Twenty-Three: August 11

Learn to love yourself, and everything else would fall into place.

Loving myself has always been a tool for building my confidence. The fact that I love the way I am is enough to make me overcome obstacles. Also, before anyone else can accept me the way I am, I must be able to look into the mirror and accept the image that stares back at me as beautiful, strong, and precious.

GOAL: Love everything about yourself and never let others define how you have to be.

Day Two-Hundred-and-Twenty-Four: August 12

At some point, you have to make a decision. Boundaries don't keep other people out. They fence you in. Life is messy. That's how we're made. So you can waste your lives drawing lines. Or you can live your life crossing them.

– Meredith Grey, Grey's Anatomy

Building boundaries are essential to making sure that people treat us with respect. But when you build them too high and give no one access, then you are also boxing yourself in. You should define your boundaries but never let it keep you from having a good relationship with others. After all, there is no complete living with having the best life you can.

GOAL: Make sure you have a good relationship with others; it can save you a whole lot of stress.

Day Two-Hundred-and-Twenty-Five: August 13

I love the smell of possibility in the morning.

– Anonymous

Every morning is a new chance to live. Another opportunity to do something right, drop an old habit, call your friend you haven't seen in ages, or develop new ideas. There are so many possibilities about a modern day that it can be overwhelming. So why not channel that energy into creating something positive and make the day count.

GOAL: Get an idea-pad, and jot down every fresh idea you get on each new day, look over the pad once in a while to see the ones you can work on.

Day Two-Hundred-and-Twenty-Six: August 14

Use what talents you possess; the woods would be very silent if no birds sang there except those that sang best.

– Henry Van Dyke

Playing the piano and listening to the classical music has always been one of the favorite things for me to do and the fact that I don't play as well as Yanni, cannot stop me from playing. Sometimes I play just to enjoy the feel of music. You don't have to be an expert with your talent, do it to add joy to the world around you. Be part of the singing bird, not the shy ones.

GOAL: Sometimes just display your talent, don't worry about expertise, the world wants to see you use what gift you have been given.

Day Two-Hundred-and-Twenty-Seven: August 15

The quickest way to double your money is to fold it over and put it back in your pocket.

– Will Rogers

There is no better way to get rich than being a prudent spender. If you spend everything you earn immediately, then there would be nothing left. You have to learn that you don't need everything that you see, it's wise to keep some money for later and if possible, invest.

GOAL: Keep some percentage of your income, never spend everything you receive for your goods or services.

Day Two-Hundred-and-Twenty-Eight: August 16

There is no royal road to anything. One thing at a time, all things in succession. That which grows fast, withers as rapidly. That which grows slowly endures.

– Josiah Gilbert Holland

Life is in phases and every day brings us closer to everything we dream of, however, it's essential to not be in a hurry. I went through a lot to get where I am now, and I didn't achieve success in one day. There were so many ups and downs. It was difficult to see a better day. But then I measured each of my steps along the way and slowly but surely I was progressing until I got to where I am. Life is not a leap; it's in baby steps that teaches you patience along the way.

GOAL: All your dreams and aspirations would come to pass as long as you are working on them, just try not to be caught up in a hurry.

Day Two-Hundred-and-Twenty-Nine: August 17

Your smile will give you a positive countenance that will make people feel comfortable around you.

– Les Brown

Have you ever wondered why you feel so uncomfortable around some people? Well, check their demeanor, and that may well be the answer. Never be that person that allows bad emotions to cloud your personality all through the day. Always be the one that lights up the room when they enter and make people feel at ease.

GOAL: Try always to be comfortable wearing a smile every day; it makes people connect with your personality and infects them with happiness.

Day Two-Hundred-and-Thirty: August 18

Relax, breathe, and roll with it.

– Unknown

Recently I travelled to a beachside city, and my hotel was very close to the beach. Each morning, I would wake up to the rolling tides making crashing sound against the walls of small cliffs on the bank. It made me think of how life sometimes throws challenges our way. If we struggle against it, we might just end up drowning in them, but rolling with it would get us to shore and safety.

GOAL: It's not every time that struggling against challenges is required. Sometimes you just have to sit back and watch life play it all out.

Day Two-Hundred-and-Thirty-One: August 19

Instead of hating, I have chosen to forgive and spend all of my positive energy on changing the world.

– Camryn Manheim

Hate requires so much energy that they keep you from seeing the good things in the world. Instead of hating what someone else stands for or represent, you should focus all that energy on making the world a better place. Stand for something and never let yourself be distracted by hate.

GOAL: Let your passion and drive for what you stand for kill any hatred you have. You are always able to find beauty in ugly days too.

Day Two-Hundred-and-Thirty-Two: August 20

Being a victim is a choice you make.

With everything that has happened in my life, it would be easy for me to sit back and wallow in self-pity. But that would not help me a bit. So I decided to turn my bitter experiences into something good, just like bringing the raw gold, passing it through fire, and displaying it for the world to see.

GOAL: Remember to do not let all the traumatic experiences that happen in your life to weigh you down, instead use it to create an inspiration to be better.

Day Two-Hundred-and-Thirty-Three: August 21

Whatever you do, never let unforgiveness get the best of you.

Forgiveness is one of the keys to living a happy life. No matter what someone has done to offend you, try to let it go. Your peace depends on it so why hold grudges. Be happy and ready to forgive no matter how bad the offence is.

GOAL: Determine to forgive everyone who has wronged you and who will wrong you. Life is too short to not be at peace with yourself.

Day Two-Hundred-and-Thirty-Four: August 22

Nurture your mind with great thoughts. To believe in the heroic makes heroes.

– *Benjamin Disraeli*

Your mind is a very fertile ground that grows whatever thoughts you sow into it. Let your ideas be about positive things, about how much you can do, and achieving the impossible. The more you think about something, the more possible it looks. This is because your mind keeps growing the idea until you see every single part of it and it becomes clearer how to achieve it.

GOAL: It's time to check out your dreams and aspiration again, pick one or two of them and keep thinking about them, write all the ideas you get about each goal in your idea-pad.

Day Two-Hundred-and-Thirty-Five: August 23

Speak less than you know; have more than you show.

– William Shakespeare

In several gatherings I have been, I have noticed something that happens a lot. Men of great wisdom don't talk much and only do when they are asked to. It's not because they are proud; instead, it's because they don't speak out of context or talk unnecessarily. The less you talk, the more you have the ability to think about what you are going to say. The same thing applies to achievement; truly, great men never brag about what they possess.

GOAL: Don't be in a hurry always to give a response; sit back, observe conversation, think for a bit, and then give your own opinion.

Day Two-Hundred-and-Thirty-Six: August 24

Defeat is not bitter unless you swallow it.

– Joe Clark

Defeat never deals a final blow until you surrender. It's just like a boxing match, if a boxer keeps taking the punches, but keeps getting up—the match is never over. But the moment he decides to stay down for more than 10 seconds, then that is when the match is truly over. Nothing has conquered you until it gets you to stay down.

GOAL: Whatever you are fighting, determine never to let it get the best of you. Winning or learning, it's both good to our progress.

Day Two-Hundred-and-Thirty-Seven: August 25

Like a fine flower, beautiful to look at but without scent, fine words are fruitless in a man who does not act in accordance with them.

– Buddha

All the words in the world won't make you a success or work magic and turn your circumstances around. I have read books and listened to motivational speeches. But what they birth in me is action. You won't achieve anything if all you do is read and don't act. So act now and don't let another day catch you snoozing.

GOAL: Motivational quotes are supposed to push you to do something. Start acting on what you read today.

Day Two-Hundred-and-Thirty-Eight: August 26

If everything was perfect, you would never learn, and you would never grow.

– Beyoncé

If there are no challenges, then life isn't teaching us a lesson, and we wouldn't learn. Without learning, we wouldn't be able to grow. We'd be in our comfort zone with no tough shell to withstand little trials and troubles. When you are facing something that seems to be big, never back down. Take it as an opportunity to grow and become even better.

GOAL: Whatever you are going through, take it as an opportunity to handle situations better than before.

Day Two-Hundred-and-Thirty-Nine: August 27

I know that everybody is so obsessed with this idea of fame, and they think that I'm obsessed. In all honesty, I'm just doing me.

– Aubrey O'Day

I have never done what I do because I would become famous or popular. And that's how it should be. Bill Gates didn't startup to be the richest man in the world. Instead, he started out doing what he loves. Passion would take you farther than ambition to be famous. Because when people are criticizing, you need passion to drive you forward, but the wrong intention wouldn't hold water in the face of tough challenges.

GOAL: Don't be driven by a desire for fame, instead let your heart be true to whatever dream you choose to chase. If it happens, must be naturally and smoothly.

Day Two-Hundred-and-Forty: August 28

Take care of your body, you need it to survive.

As much as you read and engage your mind to grow, you also need to take care of your body. Eat, sleep, and sometimes take a trip to the spa and get a relaxing massage. You would enjoy yourself more and not grow old faster than you should.

GOAL: Do exercise, eat good food, and don't forget to rest.

Day Two-Hundred-and-Forty-One: August 29

Life is more than just chess, though the king dies, life goes on.

– Tobe Beta

Things, good and bad, all have a purpose for happening to you. As long as you understand that no matter what happens, life goes on, you must learn not to give up. Give in to the gifts within you, and you would move gracefully through them all.

GOAL: Release your inner self, and you would discover you have all that is needed to face life.

Day Two-Hundred-And-Forty-Two: August 30

If we are to live together in peace, we must know each other better.

– Lyndon Johnson

Everyone around you might not have the same interest as you. But the fact that you are in this world together is reason enough to reach out to them. Don't live in solitude, always have an open hand with caution to accept people. You can't be an island even if you try. Your differences should bring you closer and your similarities even closer.

GOAL: Reach out to someone around you today, you could make flan and share with them or make some effort to know them better.

Day Two-Hundred-and-Forty-Three: August 31

Frame your mind to mirth and merriment which bars a thousand harms and lengthens life.

– William Shakespeare

Everything doesn't need to be fine before you live a happy life. Happiness should be due to your circumstances; it should be a frame of mind that you carry around each day. Try to live each day a happy one and don't let anything bring sorrow or heaviness to your heart.

GOAL: Every morning, look in the mirror, and consciously decide to be happy all day. Be the best version of yourself.

SEPTEMBER

Day Two-Hundred-and-Forty-Four: September 1

Your goals don't care how you feel.

– Dorottya

I had a friend who, while in medical school, was a victim of severe menstrual cramps that made it difficult to study on some days. However, she wanted to graduate med school as the best graduating student, and she did. The days her body rebelled against her were the days she studied more. The truth is, there will be days where the greatest enemy to achieving your goals would be your emotions or body. You've just got to keep moving and stick to the plan.

GOAL: Memorize your goals, so you become conscious of them, and they dictate what you do daily. The consciousness of your goals keeps you committed to achieving it.

Day Two-Hundred-and-Forty-Five: September 2

You will live a dull and boring life if you do not take risks.

– Anonymous

Risk-taking is an inevitable aspect of human existence. If you want to make Forbes list of world's wealthiest people, you must have a knack for taking a risk. Think of uncertainty as the bridge that leads you to the amazing life you've ever dreamt of. Thus, risk and reward are like two sides of a coin. In fact, with great risk comes greater reward. It is impossible to play life safe and expect to live above mediocrity.

GOAL: Take risks. If you come out on top, you'll be better for it. If you fail, you become wiser. It's a win-win situation.

Day Two-Hundred-and-Forty-Six: September 3

Turn your can't into cans and your dreams into plans.

– Amy Mackenzie

This can also be interpreted as 'turning your weaknesses into strengths' because it is only in our place of strength that we can truly achieve anything. Hence, when we nurture our weaknesses into strengths, we can go from merely wishing to actually execute our dreams. Embrace your flaws but do not stop here. Work on your weaknesses so that it becomes easier to turn your ideas into plans you achieve. Don't just dream your dream, live it.

GOAL: Practice mindfulness. Every time you catch yourself exhibiting a weakness, don't scold yourself. Instead, take notes first. Then, proceed to take practical actions to convert this weakness into a strength.

Day Two-Hundred-and-Forty-Seven: September 4

There is no competition because nobody can be you.

– Laureen Ben

One of the greatest lessons I learnt in life is that I am unique. Hence, my path is different from anybody. The fact that you and someone else does similar things doesn't make you the same. You have the right to display your creativity and show the world that you are unique. No one can connect to your audience like you do, no one has told the story from your perspective. Your only competition is your past self. Create what isn't existing in your field. Just do you!

GOAL: Daily reflect on who you were yesterday and make plans to be better today.

Day Two-Hundred-and-Forty-Eight: September 5

A river cuts through rock, not because of its power but because of its persistence.

– Jim Watkins.

Persistence is an essential characteristic of successful people. There are undoubtedly obstacles on our path to success. Specifically, we go through diverse challenges while striving to achieve our goals. However, it is persistence that conquers in the end. While the key to persistence is focus, persistence doesn't mean that you carry out the same action consistently. It merely means that you go back to the drawing board when an approach fails. Then, you strategize and re-strategize until you achieve your goals.

GOAL: Feed your focus and keep editing your approach to fulfill your objectives. Eventually, an approach would yield desired results.

Day Two-Hundred-and-Forty-Nine: September 6

Sometimes you need to withdraw within to repair the inner you, the layer of yourself that soaks in your experiences needs peace and quietness like a balm on the soul.

– Anonymous

There is time for everything; a time to socialize and a time to be in the solitary zone. As human beings, we daily encounter people, occurrences, circumstances that have various impacts on us from mild to severe feelings of intimidation, depression, anger to feelings of happiness, fulfillments, satisfaction, etc. Often, we end up losing ourselves in the process. Hence, it is essential (okay too) to take breaks from socializing to be by yourself – thinking, reflecting, unpacking emotions.

GOAL: Take time to withdraw from the public, relax, and unwind.

Day Two-Hundred-and-Fifty: September 7

We can complain because rose bushes have thorns, or rejoice because thorn bushes have roses.

– Abraham Lincoln

Mindset is everything. Our perception of things determines more than 100% of the outcome of our existence on earth: would we walk through life happy because we saw the opportunities in fair circumstances? Or sad and frustrated because we flee and think only bad things happen to us?

In the case of this bush, you can choose to see the thorns and flee out of fear of being hurt or see the roses, strategically navigate your way to get to the roses, and savor its fantastic smell.

GOAL: Train your mind always to see the good in difficult circumstances.

Day Two-Hundred-and-Fifty-One: September 8

You had a purpose before anyone had an opinion.

— *Špela Plemelj*

Purpose is expensive because it takes a lot of observation and investment in self-awareness for you to unravel the meaning you were truly created for. On the other hand, opinion is cheap. Everyone with a mouth and a brain has an opinion. However, this opinion is coined from what they see. In other words, people base their opinion on what you express. Therefore, do not let people's opinion of you get in the way of you chasing and fulfilling your purpose.

GOAL: Practice self-awareness so you can identify pointers that lead you to unravel your purpose.

Day Two-Hundred-and-Fifty-Two: September 9

An entire sea of water can't sink a ship unless it gets inside the ship.

– Goi Nasu

Negativity cannot be avoided. It co-exists with humanity. But, its job is to reduce a high achiever to a complainer. The best way to overcome this is to turn deaf ears to it. If not, it would drown you. Remember the tale of the deaf frog that climbed to the top of the mountain other frogs dreaded climbing? Well, it was successful because it paid no attention to the negativity the other frogs hurled at it. It focused on the task and achieved its goal. Fixing your focus on your goals blurs out the negativity.

GOAL: Feed your focus. Remember to always focus on the solution and not on the problem.

Day Two-Hundred-and-Fifty-Three: September 10

The best time to plant a tree was 20 years ago. The second best time is now.

– Chinese Proverb

If only time machines were real as seen in the hot tub time machine movie, going back to the past to right our wrongs would be a thing. But, reality checks! There are no such things as time machines. Hence, we can only learn from our mistakes and bad decisions, move on, and 'plant our tree now.' Rather than regret not sitting for that international certification exam a few years back, so do now. It is never too late to start again.

GOAL: Highlight those positive things you regret not doing, and make practical plans to do them now.

Day Two-Hundred-and-Fifty-Four: September 11

Fall seven times, stand up eight.
– Japanese Proverb

Successful people are very familiar with failure. For example, Thomas Edison failed a lot of times while trying to invent the light bulb. However, what's remarkable and consistent about Edison and other successful people is that they never refer to their failures as mere failures but as lessons learned through experience. Hence, failures are a stepping stone to breakthrough. Experiences with failure teach lessons that make us wiser.

GOAL: Every time you fall, be gentle with yourself. Rather than allowing the failures to frustrate you, let them inspire you to grow, acquire more knowledge, and recommit to your goals.

Day Two-Hundred-and-Fifty-Five: September 12

Become so busy improving yourself that you don't have time to criticize others.
– Chetan Bhagat

It is easy to point out the flaws of others and make them feel ashamed of themselves. In the process, we make ourselves look perfect, but it is only a matter of time before we get criticized by others too. Truth is, the fact that we can point out flaws in people reveals a weakness in us. We all have so much to work on as regards to our attitude and skills. Stay committed to your growth, not to criticizing people.

GOAL: Observe yourself and grow.

Day Two-Hundred-and-Fifty-Six: September 13

Start where you are. Use what you have. Do what you can.
– Arthur Ashe

Do you often feel like the gap between you and your dreams is too wide and unbridgeable because you lack the resources? As a result, you only wish you had this or that. Well, let me break it to you but once you get into the wishing zone, your dreams then only become wishes which never get fulfilled and you remain stagnant. Rather than wait to have the resources, why not make do with what you have? Start where you are.

GOAL: Figure out how to actualize your dreams with the resources you have. Resources are not limited to money. People are also resources.

Day Two-Hundred-and-Fifty-Seven: September 14

I find that the harder I work; the more luck I seem to have.

– Thomas Jefferson.

The amount of luck you have is a question of how diligent and faithful you are to your work. People only entrust their work into the hands of diligent people because they would deliver on the job. Thus, the more you thrive at successfully delivering fantastic performance at your job, the more opportunities you attract. I can tell because it has helped me build my career. Hard and smart work shoots you to greater heights.

GOAL: Get off your bed daily and commit to whatever has been placed in your care. Do not do a shoddy job; always give it your best shot.

Day Two-Hundred-and-Fifty-Eight: September 15

The key to failure is trying to please everyone.

– Bill Cosby

Say this to yourself, loud and clear, so it sinks in; "I cannot please everyone." This is a solid fact. Unless you signed a pact to be unhappy, frustrated, and to live a meaningless existence, never attempt to please anyone. Self-care is essential, and it starts from you recognizing that you do not have to do anything you are not comfortable with to get in anyone's good books. If you are not okay with it, you don't have to do it.

GOAL: If you don't like how something is being handled, speak up. Do not roll with it for the sake of trying to please anyone.

Day Two-Hundred-and-Fifty-Nine: September 16

After a storm comes calm.

– Matthew Henry

Things can be rough and discouraging sometimes. The beauty of this, however, is that they only last for a while. Although it might lead to a painful loss, the calm after the storm is always refreshing and empowering, birthing a new beginning. Although going through stormy experiences isn't easy, what keeps me going through this period is a positive attitude, a grateful heart and the hope of a better tomorrow.

GOAL: Maintain a positive attitude during crisis, practice thankfulness, and never lose sight of hope. This attitude keeps your sanity intact.

Day Two-Hundred-and-Sixty: September 17

Keep your face to the sunshine and you cannot see the shadows. It's what the sunflowers do.

– Helen Keller (Paraphrased)

The reason you put yourself down so much is that you compare yourself to the person next to you. You assume that because a person looks beautiful and free from troubles, they indeed have no worries. Well, you are wrong. We all face challenges. However, some people get out faster because they decided to focus on the brighter side; to face the sunshine and not grumble over circumstances that they get stressed out. There is always a brighter side to every challenge you face.

GOAL: Choose to see the brighter side in every dark and gloomy situation. It will be difficult, but it's worth the try.

Day Two-Hundred-and-Sixty-One: September 18

Don't count the days; make the days count.

—Muhammad Ali

Countdowns are exciting in the context of events. But, it can be dangerous when it comes to how you spend the days of your life. It is not advisable to live the days of your lives like you're flipping through the pages of a book. The secret to having amazing days is to make each day count. Pour the best of yourself into every day and make it count for something. Wake up every morning with the determination to make the day count for something worthwhile and return to bed each night filled with satisfaction rather than regrets.

GOAL: Live each day like it is your last. Make impacts daily.

Day Two-Hundred-and-Sixty-Two: September 19

You must not only aim right but draw the bow with all your might.

– Henry David

Sometimes, focusing is not a problem. We know exactly where we are heading; we have it all figured out. But, we might lack the motivation actually to take action.

GOAL: While you feed your focus, do things that keep you motivated to act. Remember that your focus determines your reality bringing many possibilities for success.

Day Two-Hundred-and-Sixty-Three: September 20

Gratitude is the seed that sprouts positivity.

– Anonymous

It can be challenging to keep a positive spirit, especially when nothing seems good. However, the greatest gift you can offer yourself is to drown your spirit in positivity. An easy way to do this is to be grateful for the things you have; be it the wig that saves you when you're too broke to plait your hair or for the meaningful relationships life has brought your way. No matter how trivial it seems, be grateful you have them. Move your focus from what you do not have to what you have.

GOAL: Practice gratitude first thing in the morning and last thing before you go to bed. Make a list of what you are grateful for, starting with 'being alive.'

Day Two-Hundred-and-Sixty-Four: September 21

Don't let yesterday take up too much of today.

– Will Rogers

Many times, we limit ourselves by the mistakes of yesterday. We wallow in the fact that we failed, and begin to doubt our ability. Or, we spend too much time today thinking about yesterday's victory rather than focus on the next big thing. Whichever describes you, understand that the triumphs and the failures/disappointments of yesterday are now history. Today brings another opportunity to win and try again. You can't rewrite or undo the past. Focus on making today's story a fantastic episode because it's all you've had.

GOAL: Move on! Begin each day like yesterday never happened.

Day Two-Hundred-and-Sixty-Five: September 22

Rome wasn't built in one day.

– French Proverb

When going through the list of the recipe for success, you would most likely find patience sitting pretty on it. It takes patience for real success to manifest. Just as the farmer is patient with the seedling to grow at its pace even as he waters and nurtures it, so also should you pamper yourself with patience and love. Success doesn't happen overnight. It is a step by step process that requires patience.

GOAL: Don't be hard on yourself. Be patient and enjoy the process. While success is the end goal, a character is built in the process.

Day Two-Hundred-and-Sixty-Six: September 23

The grass isn't greener on the other side. It's green where you water it.

– Justin Bieber

As human beings, we are all gifted with the ability to create; to make things happen and be agents of positive change. Hence, rather than searching for greener pastures elsewhere, we should reach deep within ourselves and shine our light on our surroundings. We should seek to create solutions, not flee from problems to better grounds created by other people. When you only seek to benefit from the light of others, you dim your light in the process and become too dependent on people.

GOAL: Seek to solve problems. In so doing, you water your land and give room for the pastures to grow.

Day Two-Hundred-and-Sixty-Seven: September 24

Self-discipline begins with the mastery of your thoughts. If you don't control what you think, you can't control what you do.

– Napoleon Hill

The world is abstract. I believe this because everything we see was first conceived in the mind of somebody before it became a reality. In simpler terms, the unseen controls the seen. Thus, the self-disciple begins from the mind where thoughts reside. Think of your thoughts as the steering of your actions. Your actions are inspired by what has been brewing in your mind, consciously and unconsciously. Thus, the only way to change your actions, response to things is first to change what and how you think.

GOAL: Constantly screen and edit your thoughts.

Day Two-Hundred-and-Sixty-Eight: September 25

It's what you do in the dark that puts you in the light.

– Anonymous

Ever heard the phrase closet culture? No, it has nothing to do with the fashion closet. But, it refers to what you do to prepare yourself before the fulfilment of your dreams. You can't be an amazing actor, writer, or speaker overnight. The greatest millionaires in the world today were loyal to their closet culture. They learnt skills where necessary, studied strategies in secret (in the dark) until they became an open success. Nobody ever gets anything done by lazing around. Get to work and hone your skills.

GOAL: Do not wait for an opportunity before you start preparing. Prepare yourself; opportunity or not.

Day Two-Hundred-and-Sixty-Nine: September 26

Your next chapter is going to be amazing.

I know this because we live our lives in stages or phases. By implication, this means we can always start again. We can always remold ourselves and be different from who we were yesterday; we can move from being below the pyramid to the top. This is why the dullest student in high school now runs one of the most successful enterprises today. So, if you do not like where you are today, there is another chapter. Just pick up the pen and design it the way you want it to be. The outcome is, solely, dependent on you.

GOAL: You are in charge so, begin a new chapter for yourself today. Every sunrise is a new chapter in your life waiting to be written.

Day Two-Hundred-and-Seventy: September 27

Do not react; respond.

Although they are similar, both 'respond' and 'react' depict two different acts. When we respond to situations, we let our emotions at that moment control us. We don't think, we do and say things that negatively impact us. On the other hand, when we respond to circumstances, we pause, take a deep breath, and think things through. We examine the possible outcomes of our actions before we take them.

GOAL: When you are on the edge, pause, breathe, and think things through before you say or do anything.

Day Two-Hundred-and-Seventy-One: September 28

Falling is an accident; staying down is a choice.

I was once got knocked off my bicycle to the floor by a car. My body vibrated from the thousand pains that stung my flesh. However, it wasn't until I got off the ground that we were able to see the severity of the injury and make plans to start the healing process. We all experience setbacks in life. However, it is our choice to wallow in our failure (which worsens the situation) or seek a way out. Things only get better when we keep moving. There is no progress in staying down.

GOAL: Do not give up every time you face a setback. Learn, re-strategize, and keep moving.

Day Two-Hundred-and-Seventy-Two: September 29

Don't be afraid to fail, be afraid not to try.

– Michael Jordan

It is better to fail than to be stagnant. This is because failure comes with a whole package of lessons that build your character on the road to success; it feeds you with wisdom. Stagnation, on the other hand, brings you nothing but regrets, wishes, and mediocrity. These traits are symptoms of backwardness. Note that nobody can truly be stagnant. You can either move forward or backward. Guess what? Your fear of trying is the mother of stagnation.

GOAL: Ready or not, give it a try! If you get a 'No,' it simply means, try again!

Day Two-Hundred-and-Seventy-Three: September 30

Don't be scared of labels and judgment; just be yourself.

The best way to live miserably is to live life trying to be someone you are not, to avoid being labeled as boring or a nerd or what other labels there exist. The only thing you will be best at is being you. Being somebody else alienates you from yourself, which leads to a loss of identity. We all have flaws, but the beauty of it all is growth. Growth starts with you knowing who you are. This permits you to blossom into the best version of you. Nobody ever became a unique and extraordinary blessing by being like everyone else.

GOAL: Create yourself. Reinvent yourself. Be yourself.

OCTOBER

Day Two-Hundred-and-Seventy-Four: October 1

The reason many people in our society are miserable, sick, and highly stressed is because of an unhealthy attachment to things they have no control over.

– Steve Maraboli

Several facets in life are not controlled by anything we do, and it would be unnecessary stress to try to change them. What you can do, however, is to take the things that life throws to you with gratitude. It's not about knowing everything; it's being able to make lemonade out of any lemon you have.

GOAL: Don't let yourself be stressed by those things you have no control over. Time is going to pass and things are going to be in a better shape.

Day Two-Hundred-and-Seventy-Five: October 2

No matter how many weapons you have, no matter how great your technology might be, the world cannot live without love.

– Castle in the Sky

Without love, the world would be lost in a constant circle of chaos. Love helps to keep the balance of peace and is the greatest weapon man possesses. And it must stay that way. So why not become an advocate of love everywhere you go. Spread love, preach love, and most importantly stand up for love.

GOAL: Advocate for love by showing it. Volunteer for programs that allow you to display love and affection to others.

Day Two-Hundred-and-Seventy-Six: October 3

Being strong doesn't mean that you can handle every difficult situation on your own, it means that you have the sense to ask God and others for help.

– Nishan Panwar

Strength is not defined by your ability to thrive in isolation. Instead, it is a measure of your ability to judge when you need help. I didn't build all that I am today by making myself an outcast, and I had the support of several people. The most essential things in life are achieved by groups of people working together, not one man locking the world out in isolation.

GOAL: If you are part of a group, always try to work collaboratively with them.

Day Two-Hundred-and-Seventy-Seven: October 4

When you have a wit of your own, it's a pleasure to credit other people for theirs.

– *Criss Jami, Killosophy*

Ever since I discovered that praising other people appropriately could boost their morale, it's one of the most effective tools I adopt. This is a separate thing from flattery, as that only works to put vain words to praise people. But the right compliment can go a long way in making people feel good about themselves and put more effort into their work.

GOAL: Compliment people today and watch their demeanor improve.

Day Two-Hundred-and-Seventy-Eight: October 5

I paint self-portraits because I am so often alone because I am the person I know best.

– Frida Kahlo

At a point in my life, I discovered that playing the piano has a way of soothing me and making me balance to the rhythm of the world. And this made me develop a keen interest in playing the piano. I enjoy the solitude and the serenity that the piano room gives me, and each time I observe some alone time with the piano, it's as if I'm rejuvenated. All we can do is know who we really are, invest in it, and end up being the best version of ourselves.

GOAL: Find the thing you love doing and find time to do it alone.

Day Two-Hundred-and-Seventy-Nine: October 6

I'm a warrior in steel armor, though life may offer stones and sticks, my shell is tough enough to take it all.

Criticism, challenges, tough conditions, and so much more are part of what life throws our way. But it's up to us to make sure they don't knock us own. No matter where we find ourselves, it's crucial to have a tough back and absorb pain without breaking.

GOAL: No matter what you are going through, don't cave into the desire to quit. Think about the goals that you have fulfilled in your life.

Day Two-Hundred-and-Eighty: October 7

The man who removes a mountain begins by carrying away small stones.

All the problems in life may not leave if you try to tackle it head-on. However, they would cave in eventually, if you take care of it little by little. I have learned over the years that when problems appear big and threatening to scatter things. All you need to do is stay calm, and do the things you are supposed to do, without mistakes, and it would all blow over soon.

GOAL: Write down the big problem you are facing and think of how to tackle it little by little. There is always a solution for everything.

Day Two-Hundred-and-Eighty-One: October 8

Does it make a difference being muggle born? No it doesn't make a difference.

– Harry Potter

Where we are born, what we are born as really should not be a limitation in our lives. We can choose to define our destiny and not let our background ruin the whole thing for us. Though I was from a fairly good background, I didn't let my limit be fairly good, I strove for excellence and height that would have been unimaginable had I stuck to their easy.

GOAL: If your background is holding you down, pull out today. You can have a better life story.

Day Two-Hundred-and-Eighty-Two: October 9

There are no strangers here; only friends you haven't met yet.

– W. B. Yeats

Social media have made forever growing world to seem so small now. You can communicate with someone halfway around the world with video call, voice call, chats, and so on. With all this technological advancement, we should also be able to build our social relationships. Viewing the world as friendly is key, and we must start to get to the point where we open up to the possibilities that others bring to the table.

GOAL: Use your social medias wisely, go online today and make new contacts to grow your networking.

Day Two-Hundred-and-Eighty-Three: October 10

Though no one can go back and make a brand new start, anyone can start from now and make a brand new ending.

– Carl Bard

Knowing exactly what I want to do and following through wasn't something I experienced at first, there were just too many roads to follow and all of them in confusing directions. So it took me a while to find what I love doing and pursuing it. If it's like this for you, then don't panic. Just take some time to think or ideas you would like to explore and start doing them one by one until you find something that sticks.

GOAL: Get a list of everything you would love to do, make sure you do something on that list every day.

Day Two-Hundred-and-Eighty-Four: October 11

Nothing holds the key to happiness, apart from your inner self.

Until I learned how to find happiness by myself, I was always someone with fluctuating emotions. The world won't want you to be happy, so they'll try to keep you down, it's your duty to find that inner peace that feeds you with happiness every single day.

GOAL: Don't play with your gadgets today, find happiness doing something you love, or admiring the beauty all around you.

Day Two-Hundred-and-Eighty-Five: October 12

Procrastination is the thief of time, collar him.

– Charles Dickens, David Copperfield

Time is supposed to be precious, so letting procrastination steal it is like letting yourself lose value. Don't put off what you can do today for tomorrow because when tomorrow comes, you would wish you had done it today.

GOAL: Get a scheduling notepad and try to make sure that you prioritize your time. Remember that time is the most valuable thing you can spend.

Day Two-Hundred-and-Eighty-Six: October 13

The extent of your thought is the depth of your readiness to receive.

You cannot get more than what you think of. This is because when you receive from even an eternal source, and your thought is limited, you get to a point where you say to yourself, this is enough, and stop receiving. Don't chase thoughts away from your head by thinking it's too much.

GOAL: Never think something is too big or too much for you to possess. Always think positive. Yes, you can!

Day Two-Hundred-and-Eighty-Seven: October 14

Sometimes it takes only one act of kindness and caring to change a person's life.

– Jackie Chan

A little kindness can go a long way in making things different for the world around you. Sharing happiness with someone can have a ripple effect on the day of several people. Imagine showing an act of kindness to the cabbie, and it changes his day, which would have been grumpy. It would affect everyone he picks up for the day. Never spread bitterness to others; in all, you do try to be kind.

GOAL: Be kind to everyone, even strangers. Smile more!

Day Two-Hundred-and-Eighty-Eight: October 15

Sometimes 'No' is the kindest word.

– Vironika Tugaleva

As much as it's good to be kind, you should also learn how to say no at the appropriate times. Let the people around you know your boundaries and respect it. Don't feel obligated to explain to them either, let your yes or your no say it all.

GOAL: Learn to say no at the appropriate time and enjoy more freedom, time, and energy.

Day Two-Hundred-and-Eighty-Nine: October 16

Insincerity to yourself is one of the worst things you can do.

Don't let insincerity get the best of you. You will get the best of yourself and others if you stay true to yourself. So stop fooling around and be genuine.

GOAL: Before you do something, ask yourself if you are sincere about everything you are doing.

Day Two-Hundred-and-Ninety: October 17

Worry does not empty tomorrow of its sorrow, it empties today of its strength.

– Corrie Ten Boom

Worrying a lot was a norm for me at a time where I didn't know a lot. But when I discovered that whatever would happen would still happen no matter how much I worried, I had to stop. Worry does nothing to change outcomes. They only make you lose the strength to do something about them.

GOAL: Instead of worrying, go out and take deliberate actions about what is bothering you. Take a deep breath and believe that everything is going well.

Day Two-Hundred-and-Ninety-One: October 18

A competent and self-confident person is incapable of jealousy in anything. Jealousy is invariably a symptom of neurotic insecurity.

– Robert A. Heinlein

If you are competent and confident, then it is impossible to be jealous. Because you know you have the potential to achieve what everyone else is achieving and it's only a matter of time before you get there. So why waste your energy getting jealous. Instead, you would put more effort into what you are doing and use your energy in building yourself rather than on jealousy.

GOAL: Get your idea-pad and write down the things that you feel jealous about in others, then write the things you are good at, and decide each day to try to be better at those things.

Day Two-Hundred-and-Ninety-Two: October 19

Don't waste your time on people who see you as you were instead of as you are. If they can't let go of the past, let go of them.

People find it difficult to let go of who you were before. They don't want to accept the fact that you have changed and if you stay around such people, all they want to do is to pull you down again. So stay away from them. Move with people that give you good vibes, especially if you are fighting a habit. Don't stay with those that would keep you from moving forward.

GOAL: Try to move away from people that don't seem to accept the fact that you are a better person now.

Day Two-Hundred-and-Ninety-Three: October 20

When you stop expecting people to be perfect, you can like them for who they are.

– Donald Miller

If you keep expecting people to act the way you imagine in your mind, then you'll keep getting frustrated. You have to learn how to be content with the imperfections of others. People might not meet your perfect standard, but accepting them as they are brings peace.

GOAL: Determine never to allow people's imperfection get to you, just understand and love the way they are.

Day Two-Hundred-and-Ninety-Four: October 21

If you accept your limitations, you go beyond them.

— Brendan Behan

Your limitations are part of who you are, and embracing them take you a step further in accepting yourself. Take your flaws and be at peace with them.

GOAL: Write down all your flaws and start learning to accept them.

Day Two-Hundred-and-Ninety-Five: October 22

Music has healing powers. It has the ability to take people out of themselves for few hours.

– *Elton John*

There's something music does to me at different times. It can help me lighten up my mood or help the time go by faster while I'm waiting for the train. It's like a medicine sometimes for different purposes. Music is more than art; it's a force that has the power to touch the soul.

GOAL: Update your music list and create a playlist for different activities.

Day Two-Hundred-and-Ninety-Six: October 23

God, grant me the serenity to accept the things I cannot change, courage to change the things I can, and wisdom to know the difference.

– Serenity Prayer

This is one of the prayers done by the anonymous alcoholic group before they start their meeting. It is a recitation that helps us to recognize that we have weaknesses as humans, and we can't control everything. But the ones we can control can determine the course of our life. And with the courage to truly change it, we would be fine.

GOAL: Recite this prayer every morning when you wake up.

Day Two-Hundred-and-Ninety-Seven: October 24

My mom is always telling me, it takes a long time to get to the top, but a short time to get to the bottom.

– *Miley Cyrus*

Getting to the top requires a lot of hard work, time, and investment, but staying there is even greater work. So when you get to the top, it's not the time to slack or relax and leave it all to chance. Put more effort and try to stay at that height even if you cannot climb up.

GOAL: Whatever happens make sure you are not going down. Move forward or stay put.

Day Two-Hundred-and-Ninety-Eight: October 25

If you stand for something, that means there are people who support you and people who don't support you.

– Scott Borchetta

Your values, your principles, and your way of life certainly wouldn't go down well with everyone. There is always going to be someone that would think you are not doing things the right way. But that's just the way it is. Some people would support you whatever you do and on the other side are those that would criticize you no matter what you do. It depends on you to find the right values, live them, and never give too much care about what people say.

GOAL: Write down the right values you want to adopt, and don't give them up for anything.

Day Two-Hundred-and-Ninety-Nine: October 26

Don't let your mind cower in the center of its walls, instead let it explore, dream, and take a trip to uncharted places.

There was a time I was afraid to think of owning too much, and this is because I thought I could ever get there. The vaster you think, the more your mind grows. And the more it grows, the more it reflects in your everyday life, and this is the secret of growth. Let your mind wander past the horizon and bring you tales of success.

GOAL: Let yourself dream big, don't be scared of that, enjoy the flow.

Day Three-Hundred: October 27

Be kind to yourself.

– Meghan Markle

In life, you cannot give what you don't have. And the same applies to kindness, if you have not first shown yourself kindness, then you can't show others. Get yourself that expensive watch if you have the money, don't let generosity to yourself be difficult. Start first from yourself and move to others.

GOAL: Buy something special for yourself. No matter how small.

Day Three-Hundred-and-One: October 28

You can't knock on opportunity's door and not be ready.

– Bruno Mars

There's a saying that opportunity only comes once. Well, this isn't accurate, you could get more than one opportunity, and you might get only one. However, what truly matters when an opportunity comes knocking is how prepared you are. Don't sit around waiting for luck to bring you that next big gig. Work and make sure that you are prepared to grab the opportunity when it finally arrives.

GOAL: Don't wait around for things to happen, work toward making something positive to happen.

Day Three-Hundred-and-Two: October 29

You will get what you want when you stop making excuses on why you don't have it.

– Unknown

Excuses do nothing to help you achieve your goals. I used to have so many excuses for not achieving my goals. But then I realized that was never going to get me anywhere. So instead of cooking up excuses, I started looking at what I'm doing wrong and worked to change them.

GOAL: Stop making excuses, instead work to achieve anything you set out to do. Life is too short to not get things done right now.

Day Three-Hundred-and-Three: October 30

Relax, it's just a phase, and it will pass.

Whatever you are going through, it's just a phase. As long as you are alive every day to see the sunshine and the moon set, you would be okay. When life begins with happiness and ends with joy, everything in between can be managed.

GOAL: Be encouraged by what you are facing, you would certainly get back up, just stay strong.

Day Three-Hundred-and-Four: October 31

It's human nature to start taking things for granted again when danger isn't banging loudly on the door.

– David Hackworth

A long time ago, I would only start to sort out my life when the bills would becoming overwhelming. But when they were all back to normal, I ignored what needed to be done. This is basic human nature. We only spring into life when danger is lurking. But the circle would only continue if you choose to live like this.

GOAL: Go back to your to-do list every hour of the day and make sure you are doing what needs to be done.

NOVEMBER

Day Three-Hundred-and-Five: November 1

I have seen many storms in my life. Many storms have caught me by surprise, so I had to learn very quickly to look further and understand that I am not capable of controlling the weather, to exercise the art of patience and to respect the fury of nature.

–Paulo Coelho

The more you try to fight nature, the worse things become. Imagine trying to fight a hurricane with a pitchfork and some blanket. So when like circumstances surround you, do not be so quick to jump in the midst of it without understanding it. Also, never let the hurricane get to your doorstep before you start building a shelter. Look forward, and try to plan for the stormy times.

GOAL: Make a plan for rainy days, they would surely come, but you would find it easier to get out when you are ready for it.

Day Three-Hundred-and-Six: November 2

We must embrace pain and burn it as fuel for our journey.

– Kenji Miyazawa

Pain can be used for good, and it can be the motivation that drives you to do better. All the pain of the past drove me to get going immediately. I got on that highway to success. This is because the more I remembered where I was coming from, I didn't want to return there. So I strived and worked hard to make sure I kept moving. I was the vehicle, and the pain was the fuel.

GOAL: Don't let pain keep you down, instead use it as the fuel to keep on moving. Remember that great things never come from comfort zones. Be strong.

Day Three-Hundred-and-Seven: November 3

Attitude and enthusiasm play a big part in my life. I get excited about the things that inspire me. I also believe in laughing and having a good time.

– Dwayne Johnson

Joy is an attitude that can keep you going even when everything doesn't seem to be working. Do whatever you love with joy, and the journey won't even seem so far. Let passion motivate you, jump out of bed each day, ready to take the day by the horn, and do even more that you did yesterday.

GOAL: Find joy in whatever it is that you do today.

Day Three-Hundred-and-Eight: November 4

It's okay to be sad if things don't go the way you had hoped.

– Jessie James Decker

When things don't work out the way you want, it's fine to be sad. Sadness is a chance for the heart to let out its heavy burden. But never let that stay forever, you can be sad, but also make sure that you keep healing as you are in that state.

GOAL: Remember all the times that you got sad over something and also remember how things eventually worked out.

Day Three-Hundred-and-Nine: November 5

Mire and mud would keep you down the more you struggle, but a hand would pull you out when you shout for help.

In life you always need people, the going can't get tough, and you can get stuck in a rut. The best thing to do is not to keep struggling by yourself as you go deeper into it, cry for help. Ask family and friends to lend a helping hand. I have been saved times and times again by those close to me when I was going through hard times, emotionally, financially, and that times I get down with the flu.

GOAL: Don't be ashamed to ask for help, if you are going through something talk to someone about it, it has a way of making the burden lighter especially knowing that someone else now carries it along with you.

Day Three-Hundred-and-Ten: November 6

The garden suggests there might be a place where we can meet nature halfway.

– Michael Pollan

Gardening is such a great activity, and it allows you to enjoy the magical beauty of nature. That quiet and peaceful moment that goes by as you trim the flowers, tend the nursery, and listen to the music on your player. They are indispensable, a true revelation of the peace that basking in the warmth of nature brings.

GOAL: If you have a yard, spend some time tending a garden and if you don't have it, get a flower pot and tend it carefully, trimming its excesses and watering its roots. Feel the blessing of the nature on your soul.

Day Three-Hundred-and-Eleven: November 7

To get the full value of joy, you must have someone to divide it with.

– Mark Twain

Have you ever had one of the best days of your life and there is no one to share it with? Well, that can be sad. I have had alone days and nights too, and they weren't so pleasant. So open your heart to the possibility of love, say yes to a great coffee with a friend. Life is not to be lived in solitude.

GOAL: Dress up and go to a place that you have been putting off to go to.

Day Three-Hundred-and-Twelve: November 8

Perfection is not attainable, but if we chase perfection we can catch excellence.

– Vince Lombardi

You might not be able to get the word called 'perfect' in all its essence. But chasing after it is necessary if you want to attain excellence. Masterpieces were not called so because they had no flaws, but rather that the flaws look stunted when compared to the perfection of some part. Strive for perfection, but don't be hurt if you don't get it, they are always accomplishments.

GOAL: Whatever you do, do not take your eyes off perfection and excellence would be with you every step of the way.

Day Three-Hundred-and-Thirteen: November 9

What you believe is what you attract.

Realizing that my mindset would affect how far I go in life was one of the turning points I had in my life. Never be afraid of the road ahead, instead know that you are worthy of the things that you desire. Let it be your belief.

GOAL: Your self-worth is controlled by a good understanding that you are worth more than you are going through.

Day Three-Hundred-and-Fourteen: November 10

You have brains in your head. You have feet in your shoes. You can steer yourself any direction you choose.

– Dr. Seuss

Life would try to navigate you in the direction of all your trouble and woes, but you have to regain control. Create your reality from everything you have learned. It's your life, and the beautiful thing about it is that every single day is a new opportunity for you to create a new beginning. Make good use of every moment.

GOAL: Use all the experiences and lessons you have learned in life to make better decisions for your future.

Day Three-Hundred-and-Fifteen: November 11

Staying positive does not mean that things will turn out okay. Rather it is knowing that you will be okay no matter how things turn out.

– *Anonymous*

All through my life, there have been challenges, and on the other hand, there have also been a lot of good times to remember. However, the similarity in the two of them is that no matter the one that you are going through, you have to know that you would be fine. The hymn writer said 'it is well with my soul.' Well, it's undoubtedly true, no matter what you go through, it would be turn out to be okay. No matter how long the train goes on, even when it's in season, there would be intermittent clear skies.

GOAL: Say to yourself every time you feel down. "It is well with my soul, no matter what I'm going through, it is well with my soul today."

Day Three-Hundred-and-Sixteen: November 12

Do your best and rest satisfied you have done all you need to do.

There is only so much you can do. At first, even though I tried all my best, things weren't changing. I would be sad and work harder the next day. It was difficult times, and my heart was always heavy. But everything I did then sums up how well I'm doing now. It's not always about the immediate result. Just be sure you have done your best for everything to work out.

GOAL: Never leave any day with any stones unturned, no matter the result, always do the very best you can.

Day Three-Hundred-and-Seventeen: November 13

Your mind is like water. When it is agitated it becomes difficult to see, but when you let it settle; the answer becomes clear.

– Master Oogway, Kung Fu Panda

When your mind is troubled, you might not see things clearly and make the wrong decisions. So try not to make hasty decisions, especially when you are emotional. Decisions made when angry, sad, or irritated are never the best.

GOAL: Don't take a decision when emotions are clouding your thought, instead wait a bit to cool down and look at the whole thing again. Like a day or two. You would most likely see a clearer picture.

Day Three-Hundred-and-Eighteen: November 14

Only you can make yourself feel inferior.

In your life, you are the one that matters the most, the things you think about yourself and the things that you allow would go a long way to shape your thoughts, your emotions, and eventually your life. Feeling inferior is your feeling and it's influenced mostly by thoughts we allow. Try never to feel so down that it makes you feel inferior; you are here for a reason, you are unique, never forget that.

GOAL: Tell yourself how wonderful you are and how much the world is blessed to you. You are not inferior, and you are superb.

Day Three-Hundred-and-Nineteen: November 15

Be so good they can't ignore you.

– Steve Martin

I worked somewhere years ago, and everyone loved the janitor. Not because he was funny or handsome, he was quite old. But because he was a good man. He had this sense of humor that persisted until he at least saw a smile and was as kind as they come. His attitude and aura was just really good, and everyone loved him for it. The world can resist goodness for a while but not forever. It would eventually win them over and they won't be able to help loving you.

GOAL: Be good, whatever you do, let your intentions be considerate of other people's emotion. Be kind!

Day Three-Hundred-and-Twenty: November 16

I'm not telling you it is going to be easy, I'm telling you it's going to be worth it.

– Art Williams

The road to success isn't easy, but it helps you to understand the rudiment of life when it comes to being successful. Don't be discouraged by the challenges you face on your way to the top. They are some of the things that would keep you there.

GOAL: Whatever you face in the way up, face it, and learn from it. You will inspire others too.

Day Three-Hundred-and-Twenty-One: November 17

I surround myself with good people who make me feel great and give me positive energy.

– Ali Krieger

You cannot go beyond the class of people you surround yourself with. They would secede the type of empire you would build and who you are. This is the way the mind works—it is shaped by the things you constantly pay attention to. So try to make sure that the people around you give you good vibes, motivate you, and push you to do better.

GOAL: List the people you have around you and add what value they add to you.

Day Three-Hundred-and-Twenty-Two: November 18

Hate is only a form of love that hasn't found a way to express itself logically.

– *Lil Wayne*

Whatever feeling you decide to project would cause a ripple effect. I noticed that whenever someone does something awful to me, it affects the way I behave to others. Try not to project your insecurities on others. No matter what you feel, find a better way to tackle the negativity around you.

GOAL: Hate would not get you anywhere; let compassion be the drive of your act. Don't go around spreading pain, instead just be patient and change your mood by doing something that you love. What about you doing your favorite exercise listening to your favorite music?

Day Three-Hundred-and-Twenty-Three: November 19

The mind is its own place, and in itself can make a heaven of hell, a hell of heaven.

– John Milton

Your perspective is critical in life; you can make the best of whatever situation you are in. Never see the challenges that surround you, instead channel the piece that forms the depths, and everything would take on a new light. It's all about seeing the bright side of the situation.

GOAL: Don't let the situation around define how you see the world. Remember that the right perspective makes the impossible possible.

Day Three-Hundred-and-Twenty-Four: November 20

Fear gives strength to the worst in you.

Being afraid of something means that you are giving it control over your life. You are allowing it to oppress you and teach you how you should live your life. Well, nobody wants that so why not deal with it today. Never spend too much time fearing something, instead let it go.

GOAL: Set your mind at peace that you would have all that you want in this life and let life sort out the rest.

Day Three-Hundred-and-Twenty-Five: November 21

In every day there are 1440 minutes. That means we have 1440 daily opportunities to make impact.

– Les Brown

Every minute of every day is a new chance to make the world around you a better place. You have all the time in the world to solve problems and create solutions. But it wouldn't count if you sit down and do nothing. You have to go out, volunteer, give tangible goods, and make your service available for the greater good.

GOAL: Look around you; there are charitable causes that need your help, volunteer for one today and make sure you link your life to them.

Day Three-Hundred-and-Twenty-Six: November 22

Riches without charity are nothing worth. They are a blessing only to him who makes them a blessing to others.

– Henry Fielding

Doing things for others, get your mind off yourself for the primary time. Remember how you felt every time you received a gift from your beloved ones. That is precisely how you are going to make someone feel; it's the most significant gift that you can get.

GOAL: Give some love to others today and watch as their joy warms your heart.

Day Three-Hundred-and-Twenty-Seven: November 23

A vision gives you a general direction for life while a process goal is part of the dream that you are accomplishing by taking specific actions today.

– Thomas Abreu

All my life, I always pictured myself with a good life and so much to offer to the world. And this picture guided me as I grew into an adult. I had ups and downs that shook my dreams and visions, but the picture never completely left. And at times when I reflect, it's always there as strong as it has ever been. I'm glad I never lost the big picture, and through thick and thin, it was there to shape my future.

GOAL: Live your dream, and there is no better time to start than doing it now.

Day Three-Hundred-and-Twenty-Eight: November 24

Inaction breeds doubt and fear. Action breeds confidence and courage. If you want to conquer fear, do not sit home and think about it. Go out and get busy.

– Dale Carnegie

Fear would continue to hold you back until you decide to go out and do something. Everything I have achieved in life has been by overcoming fear. Fear is a lie, and your mind would continue to believe the lie as long as you feed it with inactivity.

GOAL: Fear can keep a man out of danger but courage only can support him in it. Do something about your fear today, be brave.

Day Three-Hundred-and-Twenty-Nine: November 25

You can accomplish by kindness what you cannot by force.

– Pubilius Syrus

Kindness helps you to achieve what actions won't help you to. It is something more than emotions, feelings, or differences. Kindness is a human gift that breaks boundaries to give humanity the gift of compassion.
GOAL: Show kindness to a stranger today.

Day Three-Hundred-and-Thirty: November 26

There in the confines of your heart is the purpose you have been created for, follow its call, and you would get there.

Every one of us has something that calls out to us. Something to drive us toward our passion and push us to achieve the reason for our existence. But we can lose this voice and stray away from our purpose, and that's normal. However, we have to find it and follow it. Let the universe guide you toward your deepest desires. For now, stay grateful and enjoy the process.

GOAL: When you lose the voice that guides you, don't stay doing nothing. Do something else until you find your path again. Put a song on and meditate 20 minutes today.

Day Three-Hundred-and-Thirty-One: November 27

But let your communication be, yea, yea; nay, nay…

Integrity is important if you want to win the trust and respect of people. Don't let your words be full of empty promises or vain words. Always mean what you say and try to meet up with any promise you give to others. Also, avoid sugar-coating things more than necessary. These are principles that would make you trustworthy.

GOAL: Let your words and actions be full of truth; have integrity.

Day Three-Hundred-and-Thirty-Two: November 28

And all the colors I am inside have not been invented yet.

– Shel Silverstein

Creativity helps me to relieve my heart of any burden or sadness I have carried during the day. When I sit at the piano, it's just like the pain, hurt, and heaviness flow from my fingers to the piano and leave through the sound of music. Expressing creativity this way is a healthy and beautiful way to purge myself of all negativity.

GOAL: Look for something that you love doing that helps you release any unholy desire.

Day Three-Hundred-and-Thirty-Three: November 29

You are afraid to die, and you're afraid to live. What a way to exist.

– Neale Donald Walsch

Death is inevitable but living in fear of it won't get you anywhere. You would only discover the days and years go by while you live in misery and sadness. But living each day to the fullest is the best way to live. You would have so many happy memories. Also, you would have impacted lives around you and lived all or almost all of your dreams. Having lived life in happiness, joy, and peace, when death comes knocking, at least, you would have no regrets.

GOAL: Enjoy every day you are alive, if you think it might be your last, also remember that it might not.

Day Three-Hundred-and-Thirty-Four: November 30

Though sympathy alone can't alter facts, it can help to make them more bearable.

– Bram Stoker, Irish Author

When someone close to you is grieving, though you might not be able to change what has happened, you can show them you are there for them. Lend a helping hand, check upon them, just be there. They might not show it yet but imagine how you would feel if you know someone is there for you in your times of need.

GOAL: Show someone who is going through a difficult situation some sympathy by being there physically or calling to check on them.

DECEMBER

Day Three-Hundred-and-Thirty-Five: December 1

Think about the dawn, it would get you through the darkest night.

Life can get so bad that everything around you may seem to come crashing down. Well, This is not the time to go down depressed and sad, else things would only get worse. You have to think of the brighter days that are going to come ahead. Don't let life's ups and down tame you, instead keep believing that everything is going to be alright and it would definitely be.

GOAL: When you have nothing else to hold on to, hold on to the hope that there is nothing you can't get through. Speak to your best friend or a family member who is positive and can bring you good ideas and thoughts.

Day Three-Hundred-and-Thirty-Six: December 2

I'm flying… I'm flying! I'm not an ostrich… I'm not an ostrich!

– Blu, Rio

The human spirit has no limit to how much it can build, imagine, and create, but the mind does. You can only dream to the extent to which you allow your mind, but if you allow everything you know or is going on around you, you wouldn't dream big. Never limit your dreams to only the things you can see, let your spirit soar even beyond horizon that aren't visible.

GOAL: Set dreams and goals that scare and challenge you. Believe you can make the best of it!

Day Three-Hundred-and-Thirty-Seven: December 3

Expecting life to treat you well because you are a good person is like expecting an angry bull not to charge because you are a vegetarian.

– Shari R. Barr

Good and bad things happen to everyone, it's not partiality, it's simply life. Someone once said to me, there is nothing like a bad situation, there are only situations. It's only when you face a situation and go about it the wrong way that it becomes a problem. Whenever something happens to you, don't let your first response be to panic. Instead, calm down, analyze the situation and try to see how you can solve it.

GOAL: Don't let panic be your first response to situations, instead look for ways to solve it. Every situation has a bright side!

Day Three-Hundred-and-Thirty-Eight: December 4

There is nothing more beautiful and attractive than a person who looks who they are.

It's so attractive when someone just knows exactly who they are and doesn't compromise it. When a person walks into a room and has confidence, everyone can feel it. The truth is that looks fade, but inner beauty and self-love last forever—but only if you nurture them.

GOAL: Find your confidence and let it radiate out. Wear your beautiful clothes and your favorite perfume.

Day Three-Hundred-and-Thirty-Nine: December 5

Do it until it becomes a habit.

Habits are not built in a day; it is something that is born over repeated practice and with patience. If you want to build new habit and discard old ones, then you need to repeatedly do something good over a long period of times.

GOAL: Build good habit by doing something good every day such as exercises, new course, new language, and so on. You can set a reminder that makes sure that you don't forget and remember on a daily basis.

Day Three-Hundred-and-Forty: December 6

Haters teach you to be grateful for the people you love, hard times teach you to be grateful for the times that are good, and God, well God teaches you everything you need to know.

– Carniel Dunlop

Not everyone would love what you do and never deceive yourself into believing that they would. Instead focus on living your life and focus on what matters. Just know that haters express a form of insecurity they secretly possess, that should not worry you. Express yourself the way you want to and be happy.

GOAL: Don't let yourself be stopped because people don't like what you do, instead remember that someone is always somewhere appreciating what you do and you are!

Day Three-Hundred-and-Forty-One: December 7

You can have brilliant ideas, but if you can't get them across, your ideas won't get you anywhere.

– Lee Iacocca

Communicating with others is important if you need to convert your ideas into reality. There isn't much you can do if you don't possess the maturity and patience to work through the difference that you have with others. Imagine how chaotic the world would be of there was no good communication.

GOAL: Try to learn how to communicate well with others, it would go a long way in helping you achieve more of your dreams.

Day Three-Hundred-and-Forty-Two: December 8

Money it is a form of energy that tends to make us more of who we already are, whether it's greedy or loving.

– Dan Millman

Money reveals the greed in people, if you want to know a man's true nature, give him money. It would reveal if he has been conservative because he has no money. Money should not be what motivates your every move, try to make sure that your life is dependent on passion, love, and unconditional kindness.

GOAL: Don't let money control your intentions, let it be your dreams, passion, and unconditional love for helping others and also to making yourself happy.

Day Three-Hundred-and-Forty-Three: December 9

You create what people see you as by how you look, act and speak.

Your actions control the way people treat you. And it's important to remember that not everyone is like you. Try to be sensitive to the needs of others. Respect the boundaries that others set, there have been times when I have been tempted to treat others not to well because of the way I felt. But I have been able to stop myself and peacefully walk away.

GOAL: Don't impede on other people's boundaries by behaving the way you like. Not everyone likes a certain attitude. It's better living in harmony and peace.

Day Three-Hundred-and-Forty-Four: December 10

I think compassion is an important quality in people in general.

– Sharron Elizabeth

Most times we look at our struggles and focus so much on ourselves. But I have come to realize that there are people that face things that are worse than I can comprehend. But find the balance, don't compare the pains you have faced with others.

GOAL: Don't invalidate your feelings because someone else is facing worse, struggles are not to be compared. Always remember that eventually everything is going to be okay.

Day Three-Hundred-and-Forty-Five: December 11

Success is nothing more than a few discipline practiced every day.

Looking back, I realize that my journey to where I am now can be categorized into three basic principles—the right attitude, patience, and discipline. It doesn't have to be so complicated to be effective. As long as you are disciplined enough to adhere to the principles you have set for yourself, you can make it work.

GOAL: Get a sticky note and write the principles you would like to adopt each day and stick it to where you can always see it.

Day Three-Hundred-and-Forty-Six: December 12

There is no need for revenge. Living happily ever after is a sign that you have not let the past beat you.

– Leon Brown

The thoughts of revenge can actually seem soothing when someone does the wrong thing that hurts you. But it's not healthy, the more you think of revenge, the more complicated your mind makes it. Until you are one big fury ball waiting to explode. Let go of the past, no matter how painful, no matter how long it takes, just make sure that you are healing.

GOAL: Planning revenge won't bring you peace, it would only generate into series of events that you would regret later. Therefore, pray for them to be a better person and move on.

Day Three-Hundred-and-Forty-Seven: December 13

Laugh. Dance in the rain. Cherish the memories. Ignore the pain, love and learn, forget and forgive because you only have one life to live!

You only get to live once so why squander it on worries and boredom. Get up and do something amazing today. Don't live in such a way that you are full of regrets when you get old and wrinkly.

GOAL: Once in a while, do something for memories' sake, and live life happy and full of love. How about printing some pictures and making a nice photo album for someone you love?

Day Three-Hundred-and-Forty-Eight: December 14

Learning from your own mistakes is smart; learning from others' mistakes is wise; not learning from yourself or others is self-destructive.

– Unknown

Mistakes are meant to be made, after all we are only humans. But not learning from them is a fatal mistake and can be disastrous. Likewise, when someone around you makes a mistake, don't judge them for it. You might as well find yourself in the same situation. Judge with compassion and try to learn from them. Mistakes are lessons to our imperfection, never lose sight of that.

GOAL: Think about the mistakes you have made or those around you and learn from them.

Day Three-Hundred-and-Forty-Nine: December 15

A true hero isn't measured by the size of his strength, but by the strength of his heart.

– Zeus (Hercules)

I'm also a human being and I know this isn't referring to only physical strength. No matter the position you find yourself, never take advantage of the people under you. Whether it's emotionally, financially, or positional, show love and care to others. Let your heart be filled with love and compassion and then reflect it in your behavior.

GOAL: Make sure you treat others, no matter how much they are beneath you, with love and equality.

Day Three-Hundred-and-Fifty: December 16

Chasing the wrong things can make you lose a good thing.

– Sonya Parker

Not everything you chase in life is the right thing. You can also chase the wrong things with the right intention. It's really important to make sure that you are not chasing things that wouldn't yield any result.

GOAL: Sit down and evaluate your dreams, aspirations, and desires. Determine if they are born out of the right intentions.

Day Three-Hundred-and-Fifty-One: December 17

Beauty is about living your life and being happy with yourself inside and out and not worrying about what people think of you.

Over several quotes and many experiences, I have learned that what really matters in life is the way you see yourself. You don't have to let what others think about you define you. Be happy by loving yourself inside and out. Let it flow within you.

GOAL: Love yourself as much as you can. Do things that make you happy and buy yourself a gift.

Day Three-Hundred-and-Fifty-Two: December 18

I can't understand why people are frightened of new ideas. I'm frightened of the old ones.

– John Cage

Staying in your comfort zone should be one of the scary things that you can think about. At a point in my life, I became so conventional that it became so convenient to do things only in a certain way. But I broke the spell when it was affecting my growth. If you stay in the same place you would never learn the lessons, you need to grow and life can sweep you off your feet in an instant.

GOAL: Do things in a new way, try to think outside of the box. Believe in yourself and you can do it.

Day Three-Hundred-and-Fifty-Three: December 19

Despite everything, no one can dictate who you are to other people.

– Prince

It's good to live your life and not care about critics. But it's also important that you have a good attitude. If you don't, then people might not be criticizing you. They might be telling you important issues that should lead you to change your ways.

GOAL: Evaluate your attitude and think about what it's saying to others.

Day Three-Hundred-and-Fifty-Four: December 20

Selfish people are incapable of loving others, but they are not capable of loving themselves either.

– Erich Fromm

Being self-centered does not mean you love only yourself. It cannot because when you have plenty of something, it shows in you. So when theirs is an abundance of love in your hearts, you cannot help but share. Self-centered people are mainly driven by greed, not self-love.

GOAL: If you have always thought about only yourself then it's time to change and start accommodating others in your heart, time, and life.

Day Three-Hundred-and-Fifty-Five: December 21

Even miracles take time.

– Cinderella

In several fairy tales that we watched as kids, magic is always instant and the wave of the fairy godmother wand would change everything. But it doesn't work like that in real life. Miracles don't happen instantly, they take patience, some hard work and faith. I am in support of miracles, because I believe it's one of the things that can push us to believe in the very best of life.

GOAL: Anything you want would eventually happen if you keep working with patience and persistence.

Day Three-Hundred-and-Fifty-Six: December 22

Dream big or go home. As far as we know we are here only once, so release your fear and embrace your dreams, today!

Don't waste another second not doing what you love. Your dreams are yours for a reason, therefore, run after them fearlessly with open arms and heart. Everything I achieved in life came to me because I knew what I wanted and I went for it wholeheartedly. Having big dreams used to scare me, but once I started to achieve them I started to embrace them, and that's when they started embracing me.

GOAL: Write down every dream you have for your life. Remember, no dream is too big for you. The world is yours for the taking.

Day Three-Hundred-and-Fifty-Seven: December 23

When the day is gone and the nights are upon us, it's your face that beset my gaze with joy.

Relationship with your colleagues, friends, and family is great and you should build that. But don't also be closed off to the possibility of finding love. It's all around you, but the fear of heartbreaks or being hurt can make us stick our head into ourselves. This is a miserable way to live. So let yourself be loved and love someone so much that it hurts when they are away.

GOAL: Open up to the possibility of finding true love, no matter how many times you have been hurt.

Day Three-Hundred-and-Fifty-Eight: December 24

The right way is not always the popular and easy way. Standing for right when it is unpopular is a true test of moral character.

– Margaret Chase Smith

The true test of your moral standing is not when you measure up when the times are easy. It's so easy for me to tell the truth when there are no consequences, but when there is punishment for the truth, it becomes complex. But telling the truth in complexity would tell people what my character is truly. The best of us doesn't come out in the easiest of time, but in the toughest.

GOAL: Always stick to what you believe in, no matter how difficult it is.

Day Three-Hundred-and-Fifty-Nine: December 25

True joy comes when you inspire, encourage, and guide someone else on a path that benefits him or her.

– Zig Ziglar

Live is bigger than you alone, so when you get to the top, don't just desire to remain there alone. Try to mentor people, be supportive of those that are trying to move forward. Never let envy, jealousy, or greediness make you detest other's good news.

GOAL: Celebrate with everyone around you who celebrates, no matter how ahead of you they are moving. Remember it's not a competition, it's about being the best you can be and enjoying it.

Day Three-Hundred-and-Sixty: December 26

I myself am made of flaws stitched together with good intentions.

– *Augusten Burroughs*

We are all imperfect, no matter how much we try to be perfect. But it's the flaws that teach us we are human and we learn from imperfections to become better. This is what make us who we are eventually.

GOAL: Don't let your flaws bring you down, instead learn from your mistakes and let it move you to be better. Forgive yourself and move on.

Day Three-Hundred-and-Sixty-One: December 27

Your life is an inspiration to others, live it the best way and you would have made the best of not only yourselves.

When you make the best use of your life, you are becoming an inspiration to others. Sometimes we don't know who is watching and modelling after the things you do. So try not to live haphazardly, your purpose is bigger than just eventually living a good life, you would be doing a disservice to the world if that's it.

GOAL: A good life is an example to others, be an embodiment of good examples.

Day Three-Hundred-and-Sixty-Two: December 28

If you can't change your fate, change your attitude.

– Charles Revson

Your attitude matters a lot. I was once working for long hours with little pay, but I did the job with all diligence. When I stopped working there, my boss personally told me to come to him when next I need a job. That's because of attitude, no matter what your fate is, don't have a bad attitude. Always do your best.

GOAL: If you have a bad attitude, your fate would only get worse and if it's going good, then you won't have people around you.

Day Three-Hundred-and-Sixty-Three: December 29

Every human walks around with a certain kind of sadness. They may not wear it on their sleeves, but it's there if you look deep.

– Taraji P. Henson

Everyone has their own battles, but it is not written on their foreheads, so you might not know. Knowing this should make you treat everyone around you with kindness, don't add to the burden they already carry. Instead, make sure that they are happy and free around you.

GOAL: Treat people with kindness. If they are speeding their car, let them pass. If they're rushing around you, perhaps they're in need of something important.

Day Three-Hundred-and-Sixty-Four: December 30

No dark clouds can ever prevent the sun from shinning.-

– Mehmet Murat Ildan

Thick dark clouds have had their fill in my past. There were so many times I got so depressed because every domino that I laid to make a better day had collapsed without reaching the final goal. But somehow, I escaped all the dark clouds and even though some of them still linger, my shining cannot be compromised by them again. Life is like that, in the midst of trials and challenges, shine your inner light and keep at what you do, eventually the sun would shine through.

GOAL: Keep moving, no matter how bad things seem to be, you would eventually get there.

Day Three-Hundred-and-Sixty-Five: December 31

Dear world I am excited to be alive in you, and I am thankful for another year.

– Charlotte Eriksson

This is the last day in the year and it is time to do some progress evaluation. Look at all the goals you set and how many of them you have achieved. Assess how much you have grown, changed, and evolved. Also, try to see the way forward, these last days are not for packing your idea pad full of goals and achievements. Instead it's for reevaluating the year and then deciding on the next step to take.

GOAL: Write down everything you have accomplished and compare it against the beginning of the year.